William Hepworth Dixon, Herbert Barry

Russia in 1870

William Hepworth Dixon, Herbert Barry

Russia in 1870

ISBN/EAN: 9783337170332

Printed in Europe, USA, Canada, Australia, Japan

Cover: Foto ©ninafisch / pixelio.de

More available books at **www.hansebooks.com**

BY

HERBERT BARRY,

LATE DIRECTOR OF THE CHEPELEFFSKY ESTATES AND IRON WORKS
IN THE GOVERNMENTS OF VLADIMIR, TAMBOV, AND
NIJNY NOVGOROD, EMPIRE OF RUSSIA.
AUTHOR OF "RUSSIAN METALLURGICAL WORKS," ETC.

LONDON:
WYMAN & SONS, GREAT QUEEN STREET,
LINCOLN'S INN FIELDS, W.C.
1871.

[*All rights reserved.*]

PREFACE.

MR. W. HEPWORTH DIXON unquestionably deserves the thanks of everyone interested in the well-being of Russia for drawing attention to that Empire, and I had hoped that the perusal of "Free Russia" would have given the reader a fair insight into that country, and that from the pen of its distinguished author the world would have learned what Russia is, and what the Russians really are.

Upon reading Mr. Dixon's work, however, I come to a very different conclusion, and am strongly reminded of the statement of

Prince Dolgorouky, quoted by Mr. Sutherland Edwards in his interesting book, "The Russians at Home," "That Russians alone ought to write on the subject of Russia" (the Prince of course meaning that only those, from long residence, well acquainted with Russia ought to take the subject in hand), and also that of Dr. Eckhardt, "Still worse is it with the statements of those who have come to Russia as strangers, and who endeavour to convey the impressions they have received without being acquainted with the premises or even knowing of their existence."

It is evident that Mr. Dixon has depended greatly upon second-hand information for much of the material of his book, otherwise he could not have been led into the errors which overrun his work.

The chapters upon subjects that have been studied are not only interesting, but as might have been expected, coming from a source of observance so acute as Mr. Dixon's, are graphic and powerful; how unfortunate therefore is it that Mr. Dixon's exceedingly limited sphere of travel in Russia should have resulted in such erroneous conclusions and inferences on those questions where he has necessarily had to depend upon the information of others.

Had Mr. Dixon contented himself with giving us the first volume only of his work, then, in his interesting account of the monasteries, a subject which he has evidently well studied, there would have been found an entertaining and instructive work, to which no student of Russian life and manners could have objected; but when a writer as powerful as Mr. Dixon enters into a statement of so-called facts, and from them of deductions which are equally incorrect the one as the other, it becomes necessary for all who have studied the question, to help to place the correct side of it before the readers.

Russia is a country which, young as it is in the path of reform and improvement, cannot afford to be misunderstood; and at this time, above all others, when the reactionary party are striving to overcome that of progress, it is more than ever necessary that those interested in the subject should have placed before them none but well considered facts.

Many visits to Russia during the last twelve years, together with a continued residence in the interior for the latter four years of that period, combined with the experience afforded me as the head of one of the largest industrial enterprises in the Empire, have given me many opportunities of studying the institutions of Russia and the character of the Russian people.

Preface.

Extended travel over all parts of the Empire, both for the purposes of business and observation, has brought me much in contact with all sorts and descriptions of people from politicians to peasants. These experiences have prompted me to attempt to give a true account of those institutions *under* which I have lived, and of the people *amongst* whom I have lived, particularly drawing attention to the changes and reforms both of the people and their institutions.

It will, I fear, be found that I have omitted in this book to treat upon several topics, notably literature, military, naval matters, &c. These subjects, however, are now being discussed by far abler pens than mine, and I have been throughout most careful to introduce no subject with which I was not personally quite conversant.

No one can have lived in Russia, watched

its struggles for liberty, and the manner in which its people, so unaccustomed to freedom, use their liberty, without seeing the germ of a future importance and greatness impossible to realize.

CONTENTS.

CHAPTER I.
ON MR. DIXON'S BOOK "FREE RUSSIA" ...   1

CHAPTER II.
OLD ABUSES AND LATE REFORMS   43

CHAPTER III.
THE PEOPLE   105

CHAPTER IV.
TOWNS AND VILLAGES........................   152

CHAPTER V.
PRIESTS, CHURCH, AND EMPEROR............   175

CHAPTER VI.
SPORTS AND PASTIMES 208

CHAPTER VII.
MANUFACTURES AND TRADE 251

CHAPTER VIII.
WAYS AND COMMUNICATIONS 281

CHAPTER IX.
SIBERIA 308

CHAPTER X.
THE GREAT FAIR OF NIJNY NOVGOROD ... 343

CHAPTER XI.
THE CENTRAL ASIAN QUESTION 397

CHAPTER XII.
CONCLUSION 414

CHAPTER I.

ON MR. DIXON'S BOOK "FREE RUSSIA."

NATURALLY I have great diffidence in contradicting such an experienced and able author as Mr. Dixon; but I have no alternative but to devote a few pages to his book.

It is somewhat difficult to find out in what parts of that empire Mr. Dixon has studied "Free Russia," as from the preface I read, "My journeys, just completed, carried me from the Polar Sea to the Ural Mountains;" and at the first page of vol. ii., "My line from the Arctic Sea to the southern slopes of the Ural range;" statements which would have led me to suppose that Mr. Dixon would have studied his subject over an immense breadth of territory, rather than have chosen the very extraordinary spot of the " northern zones" as the principal place for his observations.

Unless it were to study that specimen of the human race which Mr. Dixon describes as meaning "cannibal," I cannot make out why he went so far north to find representatives of free Russia. It is not on the road from Archangel to St. Petersburgh that one can judge of the Russians under her northern latitudes; for that purpose the traveller must go much farther to the east than Mr. Dixon appears to have gone.

In the preface I also find, " Two journeys made in previous years have helped me to judge the reforms which are opening out the Japan-like empire of Russia." Why was the reader not told where these journeys were made to; and, more particularly, what was the different state of things that Mr. Dixon now found existing there?

I also read, "I have much to say about pilgrims, monks, and parish priests,—about village justices and patriarchal life,—about beggars, tramps, and sectaries, &c. &c.,—in short, about the Human Forces which underlie and shape the external politics of our time."

With the exception of the reservation I have made in my preface, I cannot admit that Mr. Dixon *has* said much about what he promises; and what he has said, if allowed to pass categorically uncontradicted, can only lead to the reader being greatly mistaken in his opinions of free Russia and the free Russians.

I presume to think that Mr. Dixon does not speak the Russian language; and, as I do not find anywhere a hint dropped of his ideas or sayings being communicated by means of an interpreter, I cannot understand expressions such as the following, which I find pervade the book :—" You hear in their speech ; "—" I asked what is this hole in the stone ; "—" In answer to my question ; " — " Yes, yes, you may hear a Mujik say." Does Mr. Dixon assume that a traveller can pass through a country, and write a work entering politically, socially, and economically into his subject, when he is unable to understand what is said to him, or to ask that which he wants to find out ? Perhaps it is to this we may attribute some of the extraordinary errors which we find in that gentleman's work.

I do not presume to criticize the book as a book, but at once to challenge many of the statements, trivial as some of them may be to general readers, but most important, if we suppose that Mr. Dixon wishes any one to have a correct idea of the country from his work.

I at once therefore plunge into that portion of the book which alone justifies the title used.

The chapter on the emancipation of the serfs is so manifestly incorrect, that it has already drawn forth the criticisms of the most powerful portion of the press; there is no occasion, therefore, for me to repeat what is so well known to all students of the question.

I can only say upon this head, then, What confidence can be placed in the statements of an author who leads us to suppose that Pensa and Kazan villages are occupied by Poles and Mala Russians?

I maintain that the peasant is the most important character to note in the empire, from the great preponderance in number of his class over any other, and therefore any erroneous ideas about him are of the greatest consequence.

Now I find in the chapter on patriarchal life the following :—" A patriarch is lord in his own house and family, and no man has a right to interfere with him, not even the village elders and the imperial judge; he stands above oral and written law . . . every act of his done within that cabin is supposed to be private and divine . . . they would not order her to be flogged—not now—the new law forbids it; that is to say, in public. In his own cabin Daniel may flog Nadia when he likes."

The whole inference to be drawn from this passage is incorrect. Everybody would suppose from it that the patriarch or head of the family, had a literal right to carry out any excesses he chose in his own home, and that, assuming they were carried out, *nobody* had the right to interfere with him or call him to account.

The only power the patriarch has in the matter of chastising is limited, and if he carries that power out to too great an extent, the person so treated can apply to the community, and the community will interfere and punish the offender.

In one village I knew a patriarch who had flogged his son, and then locked him up, so that he could not personally go and complain; but he managed to communicate with some one who went to the community for him: and they there and then sent deputies to the house to hold an inquest on the matter.

The other statement, copied from a newssheet:—" Euphrosine M——, a peasant-woman, living in the province of Kherson, is accused by her husband of unfaithfulness to her vows. The rustic calls a meeting of patriarchs, who hear his story, and without hearing the wife in her defence, condemn her to be walked through the village stark naked in broad daylight in the presence of all her friends."

The reader would have supposed that this event (if it did take place) was one of recent occurrence, whereas Mr. Dixon's authority is the "Gazette of New Russia" for 1864. To show that the authorities do not shut their eyes to excesses committed by the peasants when they do occur, I will mention one fact.

On our estate a woman had been barbarously treated by two men: the local coroner and the community shirked their duty: the matter got into the newspapers, and the next day an imperial order demanded an inquest, and the offenders were brought to justice.

How much must my opinion be shaken

in what Mr. Dixon has written generally upon the sects, which is a subject I have not had time to study, when I find, speaking of an old believer, he says—"The chances are that he will not smoke," when the merest tyro would have told him that this sect abhors the use of tobacco.

I have known a member of it, have his house whitewashed and cleaned throughout, in consequence of a man having taken a couple of whiffs at his papiross, not knowing that his host was an old believer.

Again—"Every new Emperor makes a Saint." Mr. Dixon should have been aware that the present Emperor, instead of making new Saints, has, by ukaze, much diminished the number of days to be observed as Saint days or Holidays.

Where has Mr. Dixon seen the Scoptsi (detestable sect as they are)? "White, weak, and wasting, they appear in the shops like ghosts." As a rule, with the exception of being generally rather fat, there is not much difference to be observed between them and other people.

Who, that knows the people whom Mr. Dixon calls "Non-payers of Rent," can understand what he means by calling them a "sect?" They are the people to whom I allude in Chapter IX. as those who will not pay their land-tax; and they may with as much truth be called a "sect," as that portion of the Irish population who refuse to pay their rent, believing, as both parties do, that the land belongs to them.

In "Village Republics" I read such statements as these: — "From ancient times the members of these village democracies derive a body of local rights, of kin to those family rights which reforming ministers and judges think it wiser to leave alone. They choose their own elders, hold their own courts, inflict their own fines . . . exercising powers which the Emperor has not given and dares not take away. The Starosta . . . elected for three years . . . the rule is for the richest peasant of the village to be chosen . . . an unpaid servant of his village . . . But a village elder, backed by his meeting, can defeat the Imperial will, and set the beneficent public code aside."

Now these certainly are about as pretty pictures of autocratical democracies as it is well able to conceive. Let me lay before the reader the real·facts, and show how apt to mislead Mr. Dixon's statements are. The least competent court in the village is the Starosta acting under the power of the community, whose powers of punishment are so trivial as not to require mentioning; the next court, and the one which doubtless Mr. Dixon means, is the district commune or volost, an assembly of representatives of several parishes, presided over by the Starshinar, or head man. To this court the previously mentioned one is in a degree subservient, just as the Starosta is subservient to the Starshinar.

This elected assembly, then, again elect the volost court of justice, which, according to the size of the volost, consists of from four to twelve people, three of whom sit to try cases, their sentences being carried out by the Starshinar as the executive officer.

From reading Mr. Dixon's account, any one would suppose the power of this court was unlimited; on the contrary, it is very small—civil jurisdiction under one hundred roubles or fifteen pounds—the administering of twenty-four blows with the rod—power to fine in criminal cases up to three silver roubles, and to send to prison for seven days.

The Starosta is *never* chosen for his riches, but always for his talking powers, as the community love a man who can talk well. He is also *invariably* paid for his services.

At the conclusion of the same chapter is, " Two-thirds of a village mob, in which every other voter may be drunk, can send a man to Siberia for his term of life;" and in the following chapter is explained, " Such cases of village justice are not rare," and " they can summon him to appear, and find him worthy to be expelled . . . rejected from his commune . . . he cannot enter a village." Now I object to these statements in toto. First of all, drunken people are not allowed to be at communal meetings; and, secondly, the commune has no power to send any one to Siberia. If any member of the community does not pay his dues, his brethren have the power of turning him out of the community, after having tried all other means of bringing him to reason; but he is eligible for admittance into any other commune that will take him.

In cases where a discharged member cannot get into another commune, he is sent, at the expense of the Government, with others of the same sort, to found a colony, and hence a community elsewhere; but, certainly, he is not sent to a "Siberian mine,"—a punishment kept for murderers and other great criminals.

Mr. Dixon evidently knows very little of the workings of the village communities, or he would never have stated what he does in page 58 of vol. ii.:—"Now, the villagers pretty well know the brother who is rich enough to give his roubles, in place of baring his back; and when they thirst for a dram at some other man's cost, they have only to get up some flimsy charge on which that brother can be tried. The man is sure to buy himself off." I would venture to advise Mr. Dixon, the next time he goes to Russia, to study the administration of justice by some of the volost tribunals: he will not be ashamed of the justice he sees administered there, I am sure.

So with their houses and living is Mr. Dixon as much in error as with the institutions of the peasant. I read, "The elder's hut is bigger than the rest . . . the floor is mud. One house here and there may have a balcony, a cow-shed." Where, in the name of goodness, is this general description taken from? Most positively not from Russia. Has Mr. Dixon *ever* seen a mud floor in a peasant's house in Great Russia? Excepting, perhaps, when a village has been burned, and temporary huts have been erected, I have hardly ever seen one. The living part of a peasant's house is almost invariably approached by a staircase. How can a mud floor be found on the first story of a house without the mud is placed on wood? and it is hardly likely a peasant would take that trouble from choice.

Not only what is called a cow-shed, but under the denomination of "yard," containing rough shanty for stable, place for carts, sledges, &c., in fact, the housing for the peasant's *all*, is a universal attribute to every peasant's house. This is so general, that, in speaking of the number of domiciles in a village, one never says, so many houses, but such and such a number of "yards."

Again, I read, speaking generally of the peasants, that "His dinner, on days that are not kept as fasts, being a slice of black bread, a gherkin, and a piece of dried cod." What little knowledge this shows of what the peasant does live upon: on *fast* days he does eat fish, but certainly not *cod*. I do not suppose ninety-nine out of a hundred Russians ever heard the word "cod;" the most ordinary observer could have seen what fish they do eat, and whence it comes; but the mistake is, that in this description the national dish, "Tschee," or cabbage-soup, is entirely overlooked, whilst it is the universal dish of the Russian peasant. I know peasants who eat three pounds of black bread for their dinner, and also—not one gherkin—but six.

Had I not already expressed a supposition that Mr. Dixon does not speak the Russian language, I should have questioned the statement, "I have myself *heard* a rustic ordered to be flogged by his elder, on the bare request of two gentlemen, who said he was drunk and could not drive." Now I conclude he was told that this was what the elder ordered. I cannot find the sequel. Assuming the word here used as meaning village elder, it was impossible that he could individually order the boy to be flogged; that is to say, according to communal law, he must have been tried by the village tribunal first. But, of course, people sometimes do, not only in Russia, but in all other countries, that which they have no business to do; but this fact is told us, in the chapter on serfs, as though it were the regular way of proceeding.

Mr. Dixon will excuse my saying that, if he did not see the sentence of flogging carried out, I cannot think it took place.

In the chapter on serfs there appears this passage, describing the origin of serfage:—
" A bargain was made between two consenting parties, peasant and noble, under the authority of law, for their mutual dealing with a certain estate, consisting (say) of land, lake, and forest, with the various rights attached to ownership, hunting, &c."

What can this mean? Are we to understand that the serfs wished and consented of their own free will to be serfs? If so, why does not the writer bear out the assertion which, I assume, from his statement, he means to make?

Reading the account of the parish priest and his family, is to me more like a farce than a comedy. Does Mr. Dixon seriously mean to assert that the following is a correct description?—"Each parish priest is the centre of a circle, who regard him, not only as a man of God, ordained to bless in His holy name, but as a father to advise them in weal and woe." . . . "Father Peter, the village pope . . . his cabin is very clean; some flower-pots stand on his window-sill; a heap of books loads his presses; . . . a pale and comely wife is sitting near his door . . . watching the urchins at their play . . . those boys are singing beneath a tree; singing with soft, sad faces one of their ritual psalms . . . A priest is so great a man in his village, that even when he is tipsy . . . he is treated by his parishioners with a child-like duty and respect."

It is the more extraordinary that the writer should have been led into this error, as every traveller who has noted the subject has not failed to observe upon the very disagreeable feature of the parish priest, and his mode of life.

From a rather extensive knowledge of the village priest or "pope," I find him to be, firstly, a man for whom the villagers do not have the slighest respect; a character happily only confined to Russia, of hardly any education, hardly any morals, depending for his support almost as much upon the sweat of his brow as upon his clerical duties, and is very little removed from his neighbours the Mujiks.

He lives in very much the same sort of house as the other villagers, with, however, a few more comforts in it, in the shape of furniture; his wife, differing little from her peasant neighbour, does all the house work, whilst her children run about pretty much the same as the other village children.

The pope has his land, which he farms himself the same as the peasant, and his life is one monotonous roll of church services, farming, and idleness. His drinking powers are renowned, and upon the great holidays he is invariably drunk. They themselves are not ashamed of the practice, and the people are so used to the sight of a drunken pope, that they take no notice of it, and pass him by with perhaps, in some cases, a shrug of the shoulders.

Left much to their own resources, with a very lax system of inspection, they gradually subside into a state little better, in a social point of view, than their neighbours the Mujiks, and what little association they do have is generally with them.

One great reason that kept them in this state of abjectness has been their perfect inability to rise beyond the grade of parish priest; thus one great incentive to industry, that of self-raising, has been denied to them.

I have several times seen a pope drunk when attending to a religious service, and have on more than one occasion found one stealing.

What can be said in defence of priests who would tolerate one of their number keeping a whisky-shop, and yet I knew such a one, and gave him the license to do so: he asked for it nominally for the profits of his church, but really, under the rose, it was for his own account, and curiously enough, as against Mr. Dixon's theory, this pope was, with the exception of his drinking propensities, a very respectable and better educated specimen of his class.

How is it possible that the parish priest can be as Mr. Dixon represents him—poverty-stricken and socially kept down as he is.

I trust that from the pages of this book, may be gathered what Father Peters are really like. There are exceptions to all rules, but I am afraid that Mr. Dixon's Father P—— is the exception and not the rule.

In the chapter on "Freedom" is this statement:—"This reckless sense of right and wrong is due to that serfage under which the peasants groaned for two hundred and sixty years—serfage made men indifferent to life and death . . . and the liberty which some of the freest peasants enjoyed the most was the liberty of revenge."

In order to prove this theory of *peasant revenge*, Mr. Dixon quotes the Gorski process, a case in which a man murdered a whole family at Tambof; but unfortunately for Mr. Dixon's case, Gorski did not happen to be a peasant or an emancipated serf, but was a Polish student and tutor in the family he so cruelly murdered.

This is followed by the recountal of Daria Sokolof's case, who Mr. Dixon says murdered a whole family, including a lap-dog, and " as no witness of the crime was left, she could only be condemned to a dozen years in Siberian mines."

The jury who tried her, however, in spite of a confession subsequently recanted, came to the conclusion that she did not commit the murders, but that they were committed by another person who was not found, and Daria Sokolof was found guilty of concealing the murder, and so received her punishment.

That somebody must have been misinforming Mr. Dixon very materially, is clear from the following, written in the chapter on the "Secret Police:"—"The secret police have an authority which knows no bounds save that of the Emperor's direct commands." What can this possibly be read as implying, but that the "third division" * are paramount, above all law and all jurisdiction?

Will Mr. Dixon take upon himself the responsibility of asserting that the secret police have any, or exercise any, jurisdiction in ordinary matters, criminal or civil? Does he not know that the fundamental *habeas corpus* clause of the new law is, that no man can be arrested without being brought before a proper judge within a very limited time?

What are the "third division" but the executive to carry out the order of their

---

* Appellation for secret police.

chief; and are they not chiefly, or, I may say, invariably employed in what are called political matters ?

Do not let it for one moment be supposed that I am defending such an institution as secret police; or that I am not quite capable of believing that this "third division" are even now an institution much to be deplored; and that at this day they are sometimes employed for purposes which they ought not to be; but Mr. Dixon, in describing the secret, or, properly called, political police, is saying what they were like in 1848, not what they are now.

If he refers to the new measure of law as proposed in 1862, which is so clearly explained by Dr. Eckhardt,* and which plan was adhered to in the ultimate completion of the arrangements, he will find that the

---

* In "Modern Russia."

first part ordained separation of judicial power from that of the administration; the executive power from that of legislation; the introduction of juries for hearing and trying crimes in so far as these were not of a political nature; publicity of justice, &c. &c.

I have remarked that this plan was carried out in the final arrangement which came into force in some portions of the Empire in 1864: how can, then, this assertion of Mr. Dixon's be substantiated?

The "third division" have nothing whatever to do with anything but political matters; and, what is more, I have never heard of late years of any interference by them in ordinary criminal business.

I know a good deal of the working of the new law; and although even Mr. Dixon admits that its working is satisfactory, he spoils the effect of the assertion by his statements and inferences concerning the "third division" of the Imperial Chancery; and I prefer taking the unqualified statement of such an observer as Dr. Eckhardt, that " Of all the reforms undertaken under the present Government, the remodelling of the administration of justice is decidedly the most successful," to the one-sided commendation of the former.

Such a reform as this must necessarily be of immense importance to Russia; successful as it has been, it deserves to be chronicled in all its fulness; and it is impossible to allow such inferences as might be drawn by the statements now under notice, to pass without giving them an unqualified denial.

The story of Pavlenkoff is then described; his having been exiled to Viatka, for opening a subscription to gain funds to place a stone over the tomb of the young writer Pizareff.

I am not acquainted with the facts that

were alleged against Pavlenkoff, but on two occasions my experience has been different, having been allowed to subscribe to a purse, which was being raised for two political exiles, Russians, then on their dreary way to Siberia. No secret was made of this, the police doubtless knew all about it; and although several of the subscribers were known as not having very favourable opinions towards the Government, nobody was troubled on the subject, and no objection was made to the money being received.

Allow me also to tell Mr. Dixon, that the policeman he saw in Archangel was probably *requesting* the householder to illuminate, and not saying he *must* do so.

I have always adopted the principle, that if I live and accept the protection of a foreign country, I ought in return to conform to the customs and habits of the people; and if, in fulfilling this principle, I have occasionally forgotten to do such a thing as "illuminate," I have never heard anything about it; and lest it might be supposed that being a foreigner was the reason of being left alone, I must add, that my neighbours on all sides, Russians, paid, as a rule, less attention to these so-called "orders" than I did.

From the style of Mr. Dixon's work, and what a reviewer has called the transitions in the chapters, it is a difficult task to follow the statements and arrive at his meaning.

In reading the chapter on exile, I at first thought Mr. Dixon had been in Siberia; but when I study the chapter, and read—"In one day's drive in a Tarentasse, I saw a dozen hamlets, in which every man serving as a justice of the peace was a Pole,"—I come to the immediate conclusion that he has not, for the most cogent of all reasons, that at the date Mr. Dixon is speaking about, there were no justices of the peace in Siberia.

In whatever other part of Russia the writer is alluding to, I must be allowed to be incredulous as to Mr. Dixon passing, in one day, through a dozen hamlets in which justices of the peace resided.

These functionaries do not exist in all hamlets, far from it; they have large districts allotted them, and that man must have been a wonderful traveller indeed who could have in one day driven in a Tarentasse past twelve villages, each boasting a justice of the peace.

But that they are all Poles is the most extraordinary statement of all. Even this does not astonish me more than the paragraph in the same chapter, that "the tracks have been laid down, and in a few months a railroad will be made from Perm to Tomsk."

This information is certainly exclusive—so exclusive, in fact, as to be unknown to his Excellency the Minister of Ways and Communications himself, as I state, upon the authority of the report of the Special Committee on Railways, published a few months ago, that a special commission was only just then being sent to the Oural to settle the route which the Siberian railway will take, and I think Mr. Dixon will find that it will not go near Tomsk, nor even Perm.

The most ardent desirer for the Siberian railway does not hope for its going a greater distance than from Tiumen to the Kama, to connect the water systems of Asia with those of Europe; and surely Mr. Dixon's knowledge of geography must have told him, if he had thought upon the question, that the distance from Perm to Tomsk is thirteen hundred miles; and he would surely know that even the Russians could not make a railway, piercing the Ural Mountains, of such a length in a few months. How confidence must be shaken in the statements of a book which assert in so positive a manner such impossible facts.

About the same time that Mr. Dixon was going down the Volga I was in Perm, and there they knew nothing of the railway from thence to Tomsk.

I also find Siberia designated as an "Asiatic waste," not, I presume, from Mr. Dixon's own observations. I have found several places there not meriting this description. Mr. Atkinson, who has travelled in that country a good deal, gives rather a different account of it.

The chapter on "Siberians" I presume to be one founded on information from "a Pole with whom I travel some days," not one of the most reliable sources from whence to get information on such a subject. As, therefore, Mr. Dixon does not give us that chapter as his own idea, I pass it over.

Regarding the people, I find in the chapter on " Masters and Men " some second-hand information, as follows :—" You cannot teach a Russian girl." If there is one point upon which most writers on the Russian character have agreed more than upon any other, it is the one of the extraordinary aptitude of the Russian peasant to be taught anything in the shape of work; they are very monkeys in this respect—most extraordinary imitators; prejudiced, I admit, to a great extent, and very difficult to get out of their own ways for their own purposes; but as servants, whilst lazy to a degree and shirking work, fall into their masters' ways in an incredibly short time.

Amongst the many thousands of workmen I have had under my care, I have observed amongst all classes the most extraordinary power of imitation; and if Mr. Dixon had paid any attention to the present manufactures of the empire, he would have been as much struck as I have been with this peculiar trait.

The poor Mujik has quite enough faults to answer for without being libelled.

In the chapter on "Towns" I read, as descriptive of the bazaar:—"Next to rye-bread and salt fish, saints and cards are the articles mostly bought and sold." What an erroneous opinion this is! The common people do not play cards to a great extent; and when I am told "the burghers . . . see these gamblers throw down their cards, unbonnet their heads and fall upon their knees, . . . the priest is coming down the street with his sacred picture and cross, . . . and fellows who were gambling for their shirts are now upon their knees in prayer," I hardly know what to say. That the people take their hats off and cross themselves when the saints pass, is true; but kneeling down in the streets is hardly ever to be seen: this description is much exaggerated.

Describing " Artel and Tsek," we are told as follows:—" No man not of noble birth can live in Moscow, save by gaining a place in one of the recognized orders of society, in a Tsek, guild or a Chin. . . . In one of these societies a peasant must get his name inscribed . . . if he has been lucky enough to get his name on the books of a Tsek."

I read this as contradictory; but the information is incorrect, as a peasant, a servant, *can* reside in Moscow without any such formality being gone through as Mr. Dixon describes.

In the chapter on the "Bible" is:—"A

learned Father of the ancient rite made some remarks to me on the Bible in Russia which live in my mind as parts of the pictures of this great country, . . . said the priest . . . in every second house of Great Russia, the true old Russia in which we speak the same language and have the same God, you will find a copy of the Bible;" and "in my journey through the country I find this true, though not so much in the letter as in the spirit. Except in New England and Scotland, no people in the world, as far as they can read at all, are greater Bible-readers than the Russians."

Now, leaving out of the question what the Father said, and which Mr. Dixon is therefore not responsible for, I have only to do with the statement of Mr. Dixon himself.

I have never seen a Bible in a peasant's house in Russia; I don't assert that there are not houses in which the Bible is to be found, but taking into consideration how often I enter their houses, if they had been so plentiful as we are led to suppose, it is curious that I never saw one; and as regards the quantity of Bible-readers in Russia, "so far as they can read," it is a pity that the reader of "Free Russia" was not told what number of the Russian people can read; but admitting the number amongst the agricultural class of Great Russia to be one per cent., the Bible-readers in Russia must be few. But from a statement like this, much misapprehension may arise. The reader would be led to suppose that the Russian, whom I have always held up as a model for the manner in which he carries out his religious observances, does so from a truly religious feeling, in the sense generally understood.

On the contrary, it is only an infatuation

which prompts their feelings, and an idea that by doing so they will benefit themselves; and their blind belief in a great all-seeing Power, whom they believe they propitiate by these observances. They are entirely fatalists, this is seen in every one of their movements, and they have a notion that by the single fact of going to church or crossing themselves, they are averting something which will otherwise fall upon them; but as to studying the question of religion, or knowing anything about it, I certainly maintain that they do no such thing.

One frequently sees two Mujiks in a cart or drosky in a town, drunk; one holds the other round the waist, whilst that one crosses himself as they pass a saint, and his friend does the same duty for him immediately afterwards; this certainly cannot be called religious feeling, although it is observance.

In the last page of "Free Russia" I read

the following:—" One dark December day . . . the Emperor . . . walks into the church that is to be his final home . . . the English visitors look down upon the scene within . . . alone, his cap drawn tightly on his brow . . . the Emperor passes from slab to slab."

Is this what the recounter saw himself? Was he a witness of the Emperor entering a church with his *cap drawn tightly on his brow*, or still more of seeing that Emperor, with his head covered, pass from slab to slab—those only monumental relics of his father and his father's father? If Mr. Dixon saw it himself, necessarily I have nothing to say, but if he did not, then all I can say is, that neither myself, one single Russian, or anybody that knows Russia or the Russians, can ever suppose that the head of the Orthodox Church did anything of the sort.

In the preceding pages of this introductory chapter, I have drawn attention to a few of the errors in Mr. Dixon's statements that must more particularly jar upon the minds of those who have any interest in Russia. They are questions concerning the internal life of this much abused people, that trivial as they may seem on the first blush, are so bound up with the economical question of Free Russia, that it is impossible they can be allowed to pass by unnoticed.

The other innumerable errors in the book neither space nor time allow me to dwell upon, or I might have said much in contradiction to Mr. Dixon's opinion as to the reason Russian peasants are called "Christiani," on his ideas of "Pan-slavonianism," in fact upon almost all his book, excepting the monasterial part of it.

When Mr. Dixon undertook to present a work to the public under such a comprehensive title as he has chosen, and to give his impressions upon subjects which it is clear he has never studied, then he took upon himself a task which he could not fulfil, has not fulfilled, and laid himself open to the criticisms of every student of the question, whose only duty can be to show, first, that Mr. Dixon has written very little on " Free Russia," and that the little he has written conveys generally the most erroneous impressions.

In concluding this chapter I cannot help, in conjunction with many others, thanking Mr. Dixon for expressing his opinion that the emancipation of the serfs has been a success, and thus, by his powerful pen, contradicting a very popular fallacy.

CHAPTER II.

OLD ABUSES AND LATE REFORMS.

IN no country of Europe has the march of civilization and progress in modern times been more rapid, decided, and systematic than in Russia.

The contemplation of the changes that have been wrought and are now working among the so recently nomadic populations of Russia's vast interior, by the energy and wisdom of a few master minds, will be a matter of astonishment to future generations, to whom it will prove, when fully revealed, one of the most instructive chapters of the book of history.

To the present Emperor was left the glorious opportunity of inaugurating those reforms which have led to the present prosperity of Russia.

The empire had existed almost a thousand years when Alexander II. ascended the throne, on the 2nd of March, 1855. His goodness of heart and intelligence soon began to be felt, and he quickly showed himself to be a reformer.

The conclusion of peace in the succeeding year gave him the opportunity to commence his good work. He had many difficulties to contend with: a strong and powerful party — opposed to all reforms, wedded to the system of corruption and peculation which was disseminated through all departments of the State — exerted all their influence to counteract the new ideas that, in spite of their efforts to the contrary, would get diffused amongst the people.

This party cried out against the reduction of the army; at the very idea of railways being thought necessary for Russia; bigoted in the extreme, they were against any reform in the management of Church affairs; regarded the proposed change in the law as revolutionary; and they viewed the long-talked-of scheme of emancipating the serfs as only the precursor to the ruin of the empire itself.

At least so they pretended. They knew well enough what would be the real result to themselves. Owners of vast estates, counting their slaves by tens of thousands, exercising an imperial and despotic power over their fellow-creatures, they felt that their day of unchecked extravagance and cruelty was coming to an end; and that the first breath of reform, giving, as it would, new life and energy to the common people, would lead to their ruin:

ruin, I say, for those among them who could not conform to the new order of things.

They were a powerful body, but the new party were too strong for them, and reforms followed quickly one upon the other. In those days all was bribery and corruption, the whole system was rotten; money was the only motive power; then all Government business was a matter of bargaining. If you agreed to the *price* demanded by the Tchinovnik,* you had a chance of your business going through; if you did not fall in with their ideas, the business would never move.

I remember a friend, than whom nobody knew better the ways of bureaucracy then existing, giving me the following advice:—
"Whenever you want anything done in a department, apply to the soldier who opens

---

* Government *employé*.

the door; he will tell you to whom to go, whom to pay, and how much to pay;" and this advice was perfectly true.

It was seldom that anybody refused money in those days; but in order to be sure, and not wound the susceptibilities of such a one, a particular friend of mine hit upon the ingenious plan, afterwards so well known, of placing his intended present in one side of a cigar-case, whilst on the other side were papirosses, and with an— "Allow me, Excellency," handed the case open to the man with whom he was doing business. It was not often that a papiross was taken in lieu of the paper.

The emancipation had often been thought of by preceding monarchs, and Nicholas had alleviated the position of the serfs in several respects. It was he who allowed serfs to hold land and make contracts—in fact, gave them civil rights; he also stopped the sale of serfs off the land, and would have probably even carried out his wished-for idea of total emancipation, if he could only have shaken off the feeling of insecurity that weighed upon him, caused by the revolution which took place on his accession.

He died, and it was thus left to Alexander II. to break those chains which had for upwards of two hundred and fifty years bound five-and-forty millions of his subjects in a state of serfdom and ignorance, denounced by all civilized nations as a relic of cruelty and barbarism.

Alexander II. then boldly grappled and gloriously carried out that work which his predecessor did not, perhaps could not, achieve.

When this great policy, regenerating the Russian people, was once firmly established, other minor but still important reforms followed fast, and Russia, which had remained years and years behind her sisters in Western

Europe, began to move forward with a steady progress that promises in this generation to make up for much wasted time in the past.

Although only ten years have elapsed since this great change was effected, I think but one opinion can be given as to the result attained, and that is, that it has been a grand success.

In all great changes that are carried out, some small errors are sure to creep into the arrangements necessary for their fulfilment: this was so in the Emancipation Act of Russia. There were many conflicting interests to guard, and much diversity of opinion existed as to the best means to be adopted in order to act with fairness, as well to the landlords as to the serfs themselves; and probably, had the matter been better understood and more discussed by the people themselves, the clauses which related to the measurement of the land, and which still bound the peasant to the soil for a term of years, would not have appeared in the regulations.

However, it is not my wish to discuss the details of the Act itself, but only for a moment to allude to the measurement of the land clause, as bearing more particularly upon the question as to whether the result has been fair to the proprietors.

By the Act, although the amount of land which was to be allowed the peasants was fixed from a minimum of two and three-quarters to a maximum of twenty-five acres, they were permitted to retain possession of the land that they actually held until such time as it should be measured and the legal quantity assigned them. This law being sanctioned in 1861, gave first two years, which was afterwards increased to eight, in which the land was to be measured and allotted.

Should the measurement not have been accomplished in this time, then the quantity of land actually in the occupation of the peasants was to be considered as the proper allowance, and be allowed them in perpetuity.

The official whose duty it was to see the land fairly measured was the "Miravoy l'asrednick," or arbitrator of peace, an office created by the Emancipation Act, and, in fact, a sort of judge between the proprietor and peasant.

These arbitrators were, in the first place, much too sparingly appointed, and consequently in many instances had more business than they could manage; in other cases they were lazy and would not work; and again, others meddled in concerns they had nothing to do with, and assumed duties which did not belong to them, to the neglect of those for which they were principally appointed, viz., the measurement of the land.

Proper surveys had to be made, and these, when shown to the peasants, were almost invariably refused, as, being made by the proprietors, they were assumed by the Mujiks to be unfair to them.

This, then, entailed a resurvey by the Government surveyor, which consumed more time; and thus it became difficult to get the matter finished.

The arbitrator of peace would be requested to measure the land, but frequently not attending, the people got tired of sending for him, and began to look upon the affair as hopeless. This difficulty was only felt by large proprietors, the man with the small estate getting his measurements finished in the time allowed.

By the last law, then, on the subject, all such measurements must be *commenced* in the time named, and as this commencement only required the plans to be sent in by the proprietor, the fault was his if not done.

When this measurement will be finished I do not know, but from my experience, if the Executive does not brush up the arbitrator, it will last a long time yet.

Judging from what I have seen, I should consider that the peasants on nearly all the large estates were in possession of more land than the legal quantity, and as every year whilst this measurement continues in abeyance the peasant gradually enlarges his boundaries, in most instances he has far exceeded his limit in quantity.

The peasant naturally took the best land he could find, and the proprietor is damnified to the extent of having lost his rent of it for the last ten years.

In a property of half a million of acres which I had under my management, there were thirty-six villages with a population of about forty thousand people; and when I came to have the land measured, I found that all the villages but two had more land than they had any right to, and some very considerably more. Now, all this land was cultivated—surely a sufficient proof that so far the emancipation has not failed, by reason of the peasants not utilizing the land given them,—one of the popular fallacies which is very prevalent.

I am aware that there is rather a numerous party who are apt to describe the emancipation as a failure: it is somewhat difficult to get at the arguments upon which such an assertion is founded. One of the most common is that to which I have already alluded; another is that the landowners cannot get enough labourers to till that portion of the land which has been left to them.

I do not believe that this statement is true, or that, if it is a fact, that in some portions of the empire a difficulty is found in obtaining the necessary amount of labour at particular seasons of the farming year, say at haymaking and harvest-time; it is owing to the effects of the emancipation.

Admitting that it is not to the advantage of the proprietor that he should find any difficulty in obtaining labour, I contend that, as regards the peasant, it is a proof that he has received direct benefit from his freedom, as it is evidence of his having enough employment on his own land to occupy his time.

Some may say this is no proof, as he may be, on the contrary, spending his time in idleness. This I deny. He and his family must live or starve: starve they don't, and beg they don't.

In no country that I have visited have I observed less begging than in Russia.

In the large towns beggars exist, as they do in all large towns; but even these are more of the professional sort than one sees elsewhere. By professional I mean those who beg in kind and not for money, selling what they receive.

Such a Russian beggar is always provided with a large wallet, in which he collects his alms, very generally lumps of bread, and these he regularly sells. In the country and the small towns beggars are very rare, and generally confined to those soliciting alms at the church-door; but these specimens usually are the old and decrepit of either sex.

If there is a scarcity of labour (which I do not admit), it is rather to be traced to the fact of the larger extent of ground now under cultivation.

Many of the proprietors finding that the emancipation had taken away a great part of their income, by giving them in all cases a fixed "Obrok," in place of, in many instances, the large sums which they or their intendants used to screw out of these much-oppressed serfs, naturally turned their attention to their properties, and began to farm on their own account to a greater extent than they had before attempted. Finding, as they assert, a scarcity of labour, the cry was raised that the emancipation had ruined them; whereas the true reason was the natural difficulty they found in getting sufficient hands to till the ground that had lain idle for years, and had consequently neither required or employed labour.

I have, however, a very decided opinion that the time will come when labour will be scarce in Russia, unless some plan is adopted to encourage emigration from those parts where there is a superabundance of workmen to those places where the deficiency exists.

In spite of all that has been written about the nomadic tendencies of the Russians, it is not at all an easy task to get them to emigrate; they do not like changing their homes, and no man more than a Russian loves his native village.

As the emancipated serf feels his freedom and his footing, and sees what a comparatively good position he really occupies, he will become gradually aware of the fact that he is independent of seeking other work than on his own land, that his land is enough—and more than enough—for his wants; and as railways give him the opportunity of selling his produce at better prices, and increased locomotion and intelligence teach him how to cultivate his ground more profitably, he will in time become master of his position and refuse to work for any but himself.

In the mean time, unless by some means the population may be increased, I think labour will get scarcer and scarcer.

That it must rise in price is clear, as until now the wages in towns are too high, in comparison with those of the rural population; and the establishment of good communications must cause the day's pay of the Mujik to be much enhanced.

That at the present moment there can be no scarcity of labour, is proved by the rapid and daily rise in the value of land.

In any good land district this augmentation in price is immense: land that a few years ago could be bought for ten roubles a deciatine,* is now in demand at seventy roubles; and paying these prices to farm

---

* About 2¾ acres.

oneself leaves a handsome remuneration, so that now proprietors must be reaping greater advantages from their land than they were before the emancipation; never mind whether it is owing to that fact or not.

I do not believe the nobility of Russia have lost anything from the loss of gratuitous serf labour, if the expression is taken in its fair meaning.

The nobility of Russia, or rather that portion of them who now raise that cry, did not reap their large incomes from "gratuitous serf labour," but from the incomes of their serfs who had permission to go and seek employment in the towns and elsewhere, and paid annually large sums as rent for this permission.

In all my conversations on the subject, I have found these ideas predominate in the minds of those who are able to, and do give an honest and disinterested opinion. Some of the intendants of the largest properties in the empire have borne out to me the truth of these remarks: people, many of whom have spent all their lives in what was no doubt nigger-driving, have attested these statements as being correct.

The above are, I believe, the principal facts the anti-emancipation party rely upon, and, as I have said, in my humble opinion there is not a word of truth in them. But, to judge of the real effect, and form an opinion whether this great work is or is not a failure, I prefer looking to the peasants themselves, and from that crude source arrive at my conclusions.

In all I see there I see signs of improvement. I notice new houses in the villages, much repairing of the old ones,—the fields better fenced, — the yards enlarged, — the iron tickets of the fire insurance companies fixed up on many of the houses of the more prosperous *ci-devant* serfs,—the horses more generally shod,—the more general use of iron tires on the cart-wheels,—the use of candles in the dwellings in place of pieces of pine-wood,—the men and women both dressing better,—a demand for the means of education,—a knowledge that they are protected by the law,—a better idea of what is going on in the neighbouring town,—the entering into small businesses, such as millers, tanners, barge owners, steamboat proprietors, cattle dealers, iron-masters, &c., — using rough machinery to prepare their flax and winnow their corn, —treating their women-folk with more consideration,—less living in a state of concubinage among the people.

Instances of all the foregoing are to be observed by a careful traveller in Russia.

Are they not all, I ask, a proof that the peasant is improving? And are not most of them facts which never would have arisen under a system of serfage?

I ask the reader if I am not right in my assertion, that the emancipation is not a failure, but on the contrary, a success, and a great one too.

Could such conversations as the following have taken place with serfs—but I heard them with emancipated ones.

At a small buffet on the Moscow Nijny railway, a general in full uniform (which personage in old times, was considered by the peasants as Old Nick himself, as far as his means of torture and exercising those means went) was having a row with a waiter, the man did not attend to something the general had ordered, and was giving him some reply.

" Don't you know I'm a general?"

responded the infuriated red-lined coated aristocrat.

" Oh yes," said the waiter, " I see you are, but now generals are not any more than anybody else."

Under the old *régime*, I should hardly have liked to have been the waiter, whereas under the new, he had the best of it, and the laugh was all on his side.

The other conversation was this:—Riding in a Tarentasse, accompanied by the colonel of one of the crack cavalry regiments, we found our post coachman not going fast enough; we tried hollowing at him, it was no use; swearing also had no effect; then my friend stood up, when the driver knowing what that generally meant in old times, turned round and, addressing the man of wrath, said,—

"You know, Excellency, you daren't hit me now," which had the very natural consequence of shutting my companion up, as he is one of the right sort, and was quite as much pleased as I was to see such independence, and the knowledge the man had of his newly-acquired rights. To show more fully the strength of this anecdote on the bearing of the question under discussion, I should remark that this prince who was with me, was a landowner owning an estate of some hundreds of thousands of acres, situated a few versts only from where this incident took place, and therefore well known to the peasant as being the most powerful man in his part of the country.

Who can say, then, that the self-opinion of the peasant is not improving, and is not this attribute one of the most desirable to observe in people rising from a state of slavery and bondage? If necessary I could write very much more about the improvements of the man, and the success of the emancipation, but in these pages much more will be gathered in anecdotes and otherwise, to show what he *was* and what he *is*, or perhaps more strictly speaking, *what he is coming to.*

The emancipated serf is beyond a doubt the most important and interesting subject for observation in Russia; he has been much maligned, but study him as I have studied him, live with him and over him as I have done for years, learn to know him thoroughly, get him above all things to trust you and then to talk with you, and after having done all these myself to a considerable extent, I am not ashamed to tell my aristocratic friends in Russia that I like their emancipated serf—and that the emancipation has been a very great success.

This great reform, then, was followed by the introduction of railways.

Although Russia is a country in which railways must, in course of time, become self-supporting and intrinsically profitable, private enterprise had hitherto recoiled before the map of immense distances and widely-distributed towns; and no important addition to the one railroad from St. Petersburg to Moscow would probably have been seen by this generation, had not the Emperor's Government undertaken the matter in a provident spirit, and incurred the present losses of construction or guarantee for the sake of the country and the future.

The Emperor, the landed proprietor, and the peasant, reap a common benefit from the network of lines that has now brought the capital within easy reach of all the marts, granaries, and mines of the empire, and opened convenient ports of shipment to inexhaustible stores of mineral wealth and immense tracts of excellent corn-producing land, until now cut off and isolated by their distance from the coast.

That the empire has gained vastly in military strength by its new means of communication between the capital and the distant frontiers is self-evident.

It is related that the plans of the railroad from St. Petersburg to Moscow were submitted for approval to the Emperor Nicholas. He was begged to decide between the rival claims of two diverging lines, and set the matter at rest by laying a ruler across the map and marking a direct line from terminus to terminus; and the railway was constructed accordingly. There is only one town, Twer, of any importance at all on the whole journey of 400 miles.

The country people make frequent use of the means of travelling afforded them to visit the chief cities, carrying back with them broader and more intelligent ideas than they are used to acquire in their villages.

This influence is now at work throughout the country, to the destruction of old prejudices and the general improvement of the people.

With the increase of travelling, the vexatious old restrictions on the liberty of so doing are becoming things of the past. Ten years ago, those restrictions were abominable; everywhere passports were demanded; and delays, vexation, and bribery were the traveller's hourly experience. Now the system is changed, and the same passport serves from one end of the empire to another, without interference of officials or police, or restrictions on your perfect freedom of action.

In a journey that I made a year ago over more than 10,000 versts, I was not asked for, and therefore never produced my passport at all.

The tendency of Russian policy is now in all matters liberal. In a society so peculiarly constituted as that of Russia, the introduction of any reform is a task to be cautiously undertaken. The last tariff, although decidedly protective to English ideas, is yet a great improvement on the previous one.

A steady reform is going on in the subordinate offices of the administration; the number of the officials has been in several departments considerably reduced; ancient abuses are brought to light, and, gently or suddenly, as the case requires, are swept away; and—I speak after my personal knowledge of the officials—the heads of departments are, one and all, pledged to a thorough administrative reform.

It can be easily understood that the task

of breaking through this venal state of things was an arduous one; the affair had become so ramified, that it was difficult to get to the bottom of it; the subordinates in the different offices had got matters into their own hands, and it was almost impossible to find out who was in the swim and who was not.

Vigorous measures, however, succeeded; and now a very different state of things exists.

Take as an example the department of finance which, under the honest and able ministry of Mr. de Reutern and his adjoint, General Greig, is conducted to-day as much like a Western European establishment as possible, and is a model for some of the others to follow.

The impudent extortion of the typical Russian "official" of the old school is happily impossible now. In the days when they flourished, such men would accost you most candidly, demand your sympathy with their empty pockets, large families, and small pay; explain by what process or fiction of arbitrary power they could annoy you, and leave you in the impossibility of not understanding that, unless you did "so and so" (alluding to roubles), they would reluctantly have to do "so and so" in the name of prostituted law.

An occasion of doing their duty was to them no more than a chance of extorting money; and no consideration of public safety or possible consequence was too important for a pecuniary compromise.

I found myself one summer evening in a well-known pleasure garden at Moscow, the proprietor of which believed that he had acquired a sort of English nationality in early life by exhibiting a collection of performing dogs to our late Queen Dowager, and took every opportunity of ventilating his limited knowledge of our language.

He was discussing his personal grievances with me, and in broken English said:—

"Look at these blackguards of people,"—pointing to a party of officials faring sumptuously at his expense—" after I had paid three hundred roubles for my licence, a hundred roubles for the brandy patent, a heap of money for the lease—after all this, a man came to me and said:—'I am the government architect, if you don't give me fifty roubles, I will write a certificate that the whole d——d place is going to tumble down.'"

I asked him what was his answer.

"Why, I paid the money because it was true; the whole d——d place *was* going to tumble down."

And so the matter was compromised; the architect pocketed his roubles and the public continued to drink tea and vodky at the hazard of their lives.

In justice to the venal tribe, it must be admitted that their roguery was an inevitable result of the administrative system, in which it must have been calculated, when their salaries were determined at a rate at which it was plainly impossible for them to subsist.

A judge in one of the old provincial courts informed me that his annual salary was 200 roubles—about thirty pounds a year—and "how can I live upon that?" he said.

How, indeed, he did manage to live, and prosper, with such a salary, will be probably conjectured from his next speech to me.

"Now, as you have plenty of business to do in my court, and continually have to send your clerks over here to do it, don't you think it would be a good thing if you were to appoint me your attorney? It would save you a good deal of expense and trouble, *and you would be sure to have your business done properly.*"

I believe that his mind, grown rusty in the long practice of a vicious system, did not really understand the incongruity of the arrangement he proposed; and that he was less offended than surprised by what he considered the squeamish folly of my refusal.

I believe also that he had a certain confidence in the general justice of my cause, and did not contemplate the possibility of being called upon to deliver an unjust sentence on my behalf; but it is hard to believe that my antagonists would have had a fair chance, if the arrangement had been concluded, in any case on which the arguments were pretty equally balanced.

The rigid reserve and dignified indifference to personal considerations, which we regard as the indispensable attribute of a judge, were unknown in Russia. My clerk, returning from a court in which I had been interested in a number of cases, in some as plaintiff, in others as defendant, would bring me from the judge confidential tidings of the progress of my various suits: "Such and such a matter has been decided in your favour,"—"Ivan Ivanovitch was pronounced to be in fault,"—"Michael Michaelovitch had no case," and so on—"in fact"—summing it all up—"everything has been decided as you wished;" then, "the judge sends his compliments to you, and would you be kind enough to send him a few roots of dahlias for his garden."

Such were the amenities that smoothed away the vexations inseparable from a frequent appeal to the strong arm of the law.

But not only were the favour and authority of the judge a marketable commodity; even the least of the understrappers had his dues, and levied his share of black-mail, for the performance of the most ordinary of his duties of routine.

Supposing, for example, that you entered a public office for the transaction of some matter of regular routine; you approached the proper "Tchinovnik" (who, immediately he saw your intention, began to scribble most assiduously) with a polite and friendly "Good morning, Ivan Ivanovitch." Ivan ignored you, and his pen travelled faster and faster,—repeat the salutation a dozen times, Ivan would be deaf as the paper he was spoiling. Then you would quietly lay a three rouble note on his paper, and again say, "Good morning, Ivan Ivanovitch," and inquire into the state of his health. Ivan would start as if electrified from the deep absorption of his industry, and with a friendly shake of the hand inquire what he could have the pleasure to do for you. Then you might be sure that your business would be completed with all the dispatch possible, for which, without the pecuniary incentive, you might have waited until you were weary.

It must occur to everybody, that a judge open to receive money must frequently find himself in the difficulty of being *paid by both parties*. A curious instance of that came within my experience.

I had an important case in a local court, and the decision arrived at by the judges was privately reported to me in advance of its public announcement; and it was a very awkward decision for the interests I represented. Now the judges, I knew, were *friends*, both of my adversary and myself, and they wished to please us both as far as possible.

Accordingly they came to a decision of this kind :—" Verdict for the plaintiff, with right of appeal to defendant; the judgment not to be enforced until the result of the appeal was known."

The last part of this judgment was plainly contrary to the laws of the land; and on the whole the decision would have amounted to nothing at all, as the appeal would last for years.

I sent my clerk to the court in due course to read and transcribe the sentence from the register of the court. He found it was not entered in the terms that had been communicated to me, the last clause was omitted and the judgment was dead against our interests.

By closely examining the register, however,

he discovered that the paper on which the sentence was recorded had been newly pasted into the register, in place of the proper leaves of the register which had been torn out; further, the record of the sentence had not been signed by the secretary of the court. Hereupon I questioned the secretary in the matter, and pointed out to him that, according to law, to tamper with registers or alter decisions was a Siberian affair—what did it mean?

He confessed that, when the court discovered their previous decision to be illegal, they cut out the leaves of the register on which it was recorded, and pasted in the new ones. They threw the old sentence into the stove, but, as there was no fire, he had taken them out, and, in fact, here they were!

I need scarcely add that, having brought the whole transaction to the knowledge of the proper authorities *ad hoc*, I heard no more of the second decision, and the case had to be begun over again. I never knew for certain what became of the court, but I believe they were all suspended.

The old law of evidence in Russia precluded a party to bear witness in his own case.

A curious story exemplifying the effect of this law is current in Moscow. It is related that a certain prince of high family, and who had a fastidious taste for dress, was very much dissatisfied with a suit of clothes which he had received from a fashionable tailor of the place, and he called at the tailor's house to remonstrate. The tailor treated his noble visitor with contempt, told him that he did not permit that his clothes should be found fault with, and ended the interview abruptly by kicking the prince downstairs; there happened to be nobody looking on.

The prince went immediately to the commissary of police of the district, and demanded redress. The "Quartalnik," as a stereotyped preliminary, inquired, "Where are your witnesses?" Unfortunately there were none—nobody witnessed the assault but the parties to it. The "Quartalnik" could only shrug his shoulders helplessly, and express his regret that he was unable to act in the matter.

The prince, not despairing at one failure, but steadily ascending through all the ranks of official precedence, applied successively to the fourth, third, and second police-master, always with the same result; without the production of witnesses no steps could be taken.

Finally, he went to the first police-master, repeated his case, and added—

"Now, Excellency, although I know that this tailor makes your clothes also, I have no doubt you pay for them. I believe that your aides, to whom my previous applications have been addressed, do not. I trust, therefore, that you will procure me some satisfaction for the insult I have sustained." The high officer answered, like his subordinates, "Where are your witnesses?"

However, on the following day the prince received a letter from the police-master, telling him to expect a visit from the offending tailor at a certain hour to apologize. A few minutes before the appointed time, the prince sent his servant on an errand to the other end of the town and received the tailor alone; he then locked the door, horsewhipped the tailor, and finally kicked him downstairs.

The astounded tailor, who had been led to look for a gracious acceptance of his apology, hurried off to the police-master to tell how unexpectedly he had been received. "I went," said he, "solely to be agreeable to your Excellency, believing that the prince would receive an apology; instead of that he has beaten me and kicked me downstairs, and I demand justice."

The chief sent again to the prince, and remonstrated that he had treated the tailor so ill under the circumstances, that, instead of listening to the apology the tailor came prepared to make, he had beaten the man and kicked him downstairs.

"Indeed, Excellency," said the prince, "the tailor may have told you that story; but *where are his witnesses?*"

About the last case of glaring jobbery under the old law which I heard of was the following:—

A case at law, which had lasted many years, was at last decided by the senate in a manner that would have ruined the unsuccessful litigant.

He was at his wits' ends, and had resigned

himself to the inevitable loss of the whole of his substance, when he was visited one morning by a small bullet-headed Tchinovnik, who, without much circumlocution, asked him what his fee would be if he could manage to stave off the execution of the sentence of the court. The other at first pointed out that it was impossible he could do so, as the senate had decided, and from their decision there was no appeal. "Never mind that," said the Tchinovnik. "Will you give me 5,000 roubles if I postpone the verdict for six months?"—"Willingly," said the other; "but how are you going to do it?" "Never mind that; that is my business. Do you remember our bargain?" The Tchinovnik left him very partially reassured; but in effect time passed on, and, to his surprise, he heard nothing of the verdict, and so began to believe his Tchinovnik was at work.

In the meantime he was not idle, but steadily realized his property, which lay in the Government of Tambov, and when he had turned it nearly all into portable assets he took a journey to Switzerland, "for the benefit of his health," he said. From this haven of refuge he corresponded with his creditor, and made a satisfactory compromise and settlement of his claim; after which he returned to Russia.

At the end of about six months he was notified of the sentence of the court, now harmless; and the Tchinovnik claimed his fee.

When he had received it he explained how he had managed the affair. "Nothing could be easier," he said; "it is my duty to address the envelopes that contain the notification of the sentence of the court. I happened, by misadventure, to have addressed yours wrongly to the Governor of *Tomsk* instead of *Tambov*, and, as you know, it takes, including our official formalities, at least six months for a letter to go to Tomsk and back; so the error was not discovered until the time that I promised you had elapsed."

"Did you not get into trouble for the blunder?" asked the defendant. "Not I. You see, it was a mistake that anybody might make for once—merely the direction of an envelope to the wrong governor!"

The abuses that I have exemplified in the above few anecdotes are now being fast swept away by the new law that, under the present Emperor, has already been put in force in many of the governments of the Empire.

Already the Emperor Nicholas had set in motion the machinery resulting in this immense reform, by the establishment of an excellent school of jurisprudence for the education of young men to the profession of the law. Their studies must have been voluminous and complicated, for the old law consolidated under the Czar Alexai Michaelovitch in the year 1664, contained upwards of 30,000 statutes, which were classified and arranged by the order of Nicholas.

It was not found possible to introduce the new law all over Russia at once, for the want of men fitted in ability to be the judges of the provincial courts.

Under the old *régime*, the so-called administration of justice was carried on by written forms in private sittings. Probably the greatest benefit under the new law is, that the administration of justice is now *public*, and that the superior judges are irremovable.

To every district a paid justice of the peace is appointed by election of the inhabitants and landed proprietors of each district. This election must be renewed every three years, at the expiration of which time he retires, but is eligible for re-election. He must be qualified by the possession of a certain amount of landed property. With no appeal from his decision he can inflict a fine not exceeding fifteen roubles, or a term of imprisonment of not more than three days; but subject to further appeal his jurisdiction in civil matters extends to all cases in which the value involved is not more than 500 roubles; in criminal cases, to those for which the punishment fixed by law is not more than three months of prison.

An appeal from his decision may be carried to the assembly of justices of the peace, which court may be compared to our quarter sessions. This decision is final, as in subordinate cases there is no further appeal.

Large and important civil suits must be brought, in the first place, at once before the Circuit Court, in which, besides the judges, sits the Procureur Imperial, whose duty it is at the close of a case, to give the judges his opinion of it, and particularly to point out and explain to the court the particular statutes which bear upon the case. When he has done this, the judges retire from the court, and arrive at their decision among themselves.

From this court of first instance there is an appeal to the high court of justice, and from that court to the senate; not the old senate, but a particular and special department, which acts only as a Court of Cassation, does not enter into discussion of the merits of the case brought before it, but only of the strict legality of the proceedings of the lower courts.

In heavy criminal cases regular trial by jury is established; the jurors being elected from all classes. The judges are now well paid, and therefore independent; and the old system of bribery and corruption is now impossible. Generally, I have heard but one opinion expressed in all parts of Russia, and that is, that the new law works most satisfactorily. For my own part, I can add my testimony to its efficiency. I have had much occasion to watch it at work, in the towns and in the country places; and, as all reactionary agencies are apt to go beyond their mark, so I think it is with the courts established under the new law, which are apt to exaggerate beyond the limits of strict justice the indulgence they show to the poor man in his occasional disputes with his wealthy neighbours. But this temporary evil will subside with the novelty of the changes that have been effected.

It is a better error than the former evil, when an observant writer on Russian policy remarked, — The administration of justice was indeed the department most requiring reform; for of no country could it be more truly said that "there is one law for the poor, and another for the rich."

I have known the time when a man of high military rank would literally override everything and everybody in a so-called court of justice; now such a one is no better than his neighbour, and before a justice of the peace the Mujik receives the same justice as the gentleman.

Under the old *régime*, the long delays of the law, in criminal as well as in civil courts, were notorious. Now, the decisions are so prompt, that the peasants are bewildered. I had occasion recently to prosecute a peasant for stealing staves. He was found guilty, and condemned to three months' imprisonment. The day after the trial, his wife came to me, to ask me how much a week I should allow her for the term of her husband's imprisonment. I was astonished at such a request, and I asked her, "Don't you think he deserved it?" "Yes," she said, "he certainly stole the staves; but the matter has been decided so quickly, that my husband has had no time to arrange his affairs before he was sent away to prison."

If the Minister of Justice should ever read that anecdote, it will tell him volumes of the superior efficiency of the new law to the old.

There is a great want of clever advocates in Russia; as, until 1862, any free man could act as an advocate before any court. The chief cities are fairly provided with clever and educated men of this profession, and *some* among them are scrupulously honest. While I write, I am reminded of such an exceptional advocate of Moscow, who has often advised me in intricate matters, and aroused my admiration, not alone for his great talents and his perfect knowledge of his own law, but for his equal familiarity with the laws of foreign countries, especially our own.

But in the country towns, a good lawyer was rarely to be found. There was no distinction of solicitor and advocate as with us, and nothing in the rules of the profession prevented the most ignorant of men adopting it at their own pleasure.

Advocates attached to the courts established by the new law, that is, to the Circuit Courts, or the Supreme Courts, are now sworn in; and facilities for pleading on behalf of their clients are allowed them, which are withheld from strangers practising as advocates.

I remember, a few months back, that my attention was called to a drunken and loquacious lawyer, at a public traktir in Nijny Novgorod, who was exhibiting to the company his client's papers, powers of attorney, and such things, and boasting of his influence in the courts. The man's appearance fully confirmed what I was told of his station in life—he was a simple Mujik.

A remarkable advance in the principle, long since an element of Russian society, of local self-government, has been made by the institution of certain elected bodies called district assemblies. One of these elected assemblies is established in every district, and may be described as combining the functions of our vestries and Board of Works. It looks after the roads, bridges, distribution of state taxes amongst the population, &c., and sends some of its members to the provincial assembly, which looks after the general business of the province, such as imposing taxes, attending to hospitals, prisons, doctors, &c.

Local self-government is no new responsibility for the Russian peasant, in theory, however much the abuse of power may have trammelled him hitherto in its practical enjoyment, and the working of the new system of Zemstvoes is found to be improving, although it must be admitted that at present they have not done much. In some provinces they have been able to come to the assistance of the Government by supporting a share of the burdens of the guarantee, by means of which the capital has been raised for the railways.

It is abundantly evident that the liberal measures of the Government have inspired confidence in the people. Many significant facts prove this.

A few years ago, the peasantry hoarded their savings in their own possession, having no faith in the security of the Government funds. Now, these savings of years are being brought to daylight, and the investments of the peasantry have already produced a notable effect on the value of the imperial securities.

The produce of the soil is improved in value by the new facilities of transport that the railways afford. The small farmer (and all Russian peasants under the communal system are small farmers) perceives that his cereals fetch a better price in a distant market than they do in the neighbouring bazaar. This discovery puts into his head an idea of trading; he combines with his neighbours to carry it out, and frequently prospers beyond his most sanguine expectations. I know many men, formerly of the lowest peasant class, who are now become the heads of really important mercantile concerns.

An important lesson that all Russians have still to learn, and that probably nothing but railway travelling will teach them, is the value of time. I was travelling once on the railway from Nijny Novgorod to Moscow, and happened to remark to a fellow-passenger that the train was two hours behind time. He appeared to be quite astonished at my noticing such a trifle, and, after a puzzled pause, replied, "What possible difference can it make to you and me if we get to Moscow to-day or to-morrow?"

Generally, manufactures and trade prosper and increase under the new *régime:* the people are becoming intelligent and apt to imbibe new ideas; newspapers are more numerous, and more generally read, than they used to be. One hears much free discussion of politics and the acts of the Government; the masses are being aroused to watchfulness of their own interests; and the old lethargy of despondency that a few years ago was so characteristic of the Russian character is altogether gone.

It is instructive to watch the annual improvement of the budget during the past few years. In spite of the large annual amount—nearly thirteen millions sterling—required for the payment of interest on the national debt, and setting aside extraordinary receipts and extraordinary expenditure, the deficit on the rest of the account is now not so important, and is diminishing year by year.

If Russia can only remain at peace for a few years, her development must assuredly be extraordinary.

This country, so rich in natural resources, with her mineral wealth as yet unexplored, her almost unlimited corn-producing power, and her vast steppes of incalculable acreage of pasture-land for cattle, requires only the blessing of peace to be, under her present liberally inclined Government, fully opened up. What the future destiny of the mighty Empire will be few can judge. With her resources such as I have mentioned, her system of making herself gradually independent of other countries by the extension of her own manufacturing power, she is marching onwards rapidly yet surely; and few people, who have not travelled much over the country, have any idea of what she is doing. Russia is now making her own rails in more places than one; several manufactories exist for building railway waggons; contracts have been undertaken by native Russian subjects for the building of locomotives: and the day is not far off when Russian-built locomotives will be running on Russian railways.

Government do all they can to foster and encourage the increase of manufactories. The restrictions that formerly harassed the employer of labour and fettered trade, are rapidly being abolished.

The Government itself, which was a large manufacturer and producer (particularly of metals), is transferring its interests to private, therefore to more judicious and profitable management than its own; and the principle is now thoroughly established in the Empire, that *government* and not *commerce* is the proper occupation of the Crown.

A great field is opening up in Russia for the immigration of foreign labour and enterprise. In former years there was always a certain risk attached to foreign undertakings; they were regarded with disfavour, subjected to severe restrictions, and occasionally suffered severely from the injustice that was the rule of official business rather than the occasional exception. Now, on the contrary, their rights and liberties are as safe as at home; they are favoured and protected, encouraged to set the example of intelligent perseverance to the natives, who follow in the track with much alacrity when they are shown how money is to be made.

I have made the acquaintance of many English, Germans, and others now settled in Russia, who, having come over as working mechanics, or, at best, as foremen to works, have all achieved independence, and many, great wealth in the country, and are now engaged in large undertakings on their own account.

An Englishman, settled in Tiumen, said to me the other day, "Yes, I have just come from a visit to the old country; but I like Russia best. I was a foreman in Glasgow seven years ago, when I had the offer of coming here. I wanted to better myself, and I came. Well, I have not done so badly over here; I have just given up my situation, and I have got 15,000 roubles in the bank of my own, and now I am going into building steamboats, which I mean to run on the Siberian rivers."

This man would have been a long time accumulating £2,000 as an engineer's foreman in Glasgow.

A sign of the change that is working among the people, of their steady advance in intelligence and prudence, is the recent increase in the practice of life and fire insurance throughout the country.

Fire insurance has now become more the rule, as may be seen in passing among houses and other buildings in far-away parts, by the metal badges of the companies nailed to the walls. In the old times the people had a strong religious prejudice against insurance; they said it was mistrusting Providence.

In those days, when a fire broke out in a village, the custom of the people was first to remove their pictures of the saints, then their little quantity of household goods, take the windows out of the houses, and so let the whole village blaze away;—while they stood looking on with their hands folded, and exclaimed, in their own language, "It is the act of God!" This happened often within my own experience. Once, when I found the priest and all the people quietly looking on at a large fire close to a lake, I asked the "pope" why he was not trying to put the fire out. "No use to try that," he said, "it is the act of God." "Well," I said, "I will try what I can do;" and, in effect, under my orders, the people put the fire out before very much damage was done. Next morning I met the pope, and said to him:—"Well, you see we put that fire out last night." "Oh, no," he said, "not you; it was the act of God!"

CHAPTER III.

THE PEOPLE.

BEFORE the emancipation there were only two classes of people in Russia—the nobles and the serfs, excepting always the foreigners in the great towns. As Bishop James, in his "Journal of a Tour in 1813," says:—"Looking to society in Russia, we shall find there exist in fact only two distinct classes, the nobles and the slaves." This is altered now, and we may divide the native population into at least five classes:—1. The high aristocracy; 2. The landowners, or common nobility;

3. The merchants, who have adopted French ways of living and thinking, in imitation of the aristocracy, and thus, as it were, de-Russianized themselves; 4. The native merchants and tradesmen, who retain the manners of their ancestors; 5. The peasantry.

The first class is, in my opinion, a useless, effete order of men. In spite of their elaborate system of education, there are but few individuals among them who write their mark on society. They all speak a number of languages with fluency; they bow with an extraordinary grace that would do credit to a dancing-master; they are superficially polite, and versed in the shibboleths of the fashionable world; they are great connoisseurs of wine, horses, operas, and such things; and epicures in eating, dressing, and furnishing; but there is little that is manly or earnest in the race; and generations of luxury and vanity have turned their blood to water. Brought up from the cradle in luxurious and effeminate habits, they never shake these off in after-life.

Their schoolboys are pasty-faced dolls—over-dressed little swells, in polished boots and glossy clothes, for which they shudder at a drop of rain. When I think of the healthy schoolboy life of home, it makes me pity these poor little mannikins, who trot about the streets in the hands of a governess, who lectures them everlastingly on the proprieties. The boys are so like girls that there is nothing to say of these last, excepting perhaps that they are more so. As a result they form a frivolous and immoral society, a useless and costly excrescence on the social body. In the reign of the late Emperor, every young man was obliged to serve in one or other of the employments of the Government; now this is no longer compulsory, although regarded as the proper thing to do.

The favourite branch of the service for the youths of noble family is the Guards, whose occupation it is, in handsome uniform and equipments, to play at soldiers in the capital for their work, and to kill time in their more laborious hours of pleasure.

They are to be seen in multitudes at all places of fashionable amusement,—and without them neither opera, concert, nor ball is attractive to the upper class.

These spoilt children of fortune have an amiable trait of their character, and more agreeable companions by road or rail it would be difficult to meet. They are courteous and friendly to foreigners, however haughtily disposed to their countrymen; well informed, too, in a certain way—that is, in matters relating to the lighter interests of humanity, which are the business of their lives. The politics of the Jockey Club and the opera-house, for them fill the place of more serious matters of interest, and they are nearly all excellent players at games of chance and skill. But it would be rash to ask or expect from them information about the antiquities or history of their country, its frontier possessions, or internal resources. They would give no better answer than my postboy did, when I asked him about an old Tartar earthwork, near Kosloff, that he passed every day of his life, that his forefathers probably helped to make "under the knout." It was a long, low embankment, with a dry moat at the foot, as plainly man's work as a brick house, but he only knew of it as a "little hill."

The better sort are not blind to the imperfections of the system of education, that ends in the accomplishments of the ballroom and the court, and they were well advised

by a learned man high in office when, a year or two since, making a visit of inspection at the University of Kertch, he said:—
"Gentlemen, see if you cannot educate your young men to make them more like men. The present generation, I admit, are, superficially, very intelligent. They are very polite, make a very good appearance in a ball-room, talk excellent French and other modern languages; but in spite of all this, they positively know nothing at all. Talk to them, and you will see that the majority are, according to the ideas of the other civilized nations of the world, not educated at all. Now, gentlemen, teach them a little more Latin, Greek, and history, and make men of them!"

In some houses where the claims of society are less acknowledged, the fashion of education falls into the opposite extreme, and we find little pedants of ten years old at their book from morning to night, to the destruction of their health and the confusion of their mental faculties. Both boys and girls are launched into society at an early age, and from the date of that event "society" claims them utterly, to the exclusion of all solid national pursuits.

There are but a few learned societies in St. Petersburg, but the members of the aristocracy who belong to them are not numerous.

The population of every country town always includes a large number of persons having more or less claim to the designation of noblemen. Their abundance is more ridiculous here than in Germany. Everybody who held freehold land was formerly noble, and all their children and descendants continue *noble* to the end of time.

As a consequence, multitudes of a low position in the social scale claim the distinction; and, to add to the crowd, every Tchinovnik or servant of the Crown is noble also by virtue of his office; so also do certain distinctions at the universities achieve nobility.

The Tchinovniks, educated in the gymnasium or public school of their district, are not eminent either for learning or intelligence. These men seldom know any language but Russian, or anything else but the routine of their duties and a few games of cards. They eat enormously, sleep profoundly and perpetually, and devote their waking moments to gambling or the local theatres.

They are (less now than formerly) a proud and exclusive set, disdaining the society of the merchant class, whose admission to the nobility club used to be rigorously prohibited. The ladies of this exclusive set, not having the resources of a club or even a nominal employment, lead, if possible, a lazier, more listless life than their husbands. What they find to do besides eating, sleeping, and talking scandal, they alone know. I have been frequently in their houses, and I seldom or never saw a book in their possession; a library, or any collection of books, is an object of astonishment to them.

When it is remembered how principal a part modern languages form of all education in Russia, and that these Tchinovniks abound in all country-towns, being in fact the Government officials of their respective quarters, it will be seen that the picture I have drawn of their want of education is not over-coloured from the following incident.

A friend on his way to visit me, was stopped in his journey by a river, which had reached that stage of congelation at which it can be crossed neither in a boat nor sledge —the ice, obstructing the water, and yet being too weak to support a man's weight—my friend had to wait for the effects of another day of frost before venturing to continue his journey, but he could speak no word of Russian, and had important need of an interpreter. Under these circumstances the whole town was searched for one, and it was only after repeated attempts that at last a French lady, a governess in a family, was discovered; not one of the Tchinovnicks, nor their families, being able to interpret a few words of French, German, or English.

I know the town well. Among its 15,000 inhabitants I believe there are, at most, three or four who can speak the French language.

To close my remarks about the aristocracy of Russia, I quote one of the most learned professors in the city of Moscow, who said to me, " the Russian aristocracy have all the worst vices of the French grafted on to their native barbarism." I believe this is too severe a censure to pass on a whole class, among which must be found many amiable and highly intelligent individuals, but I quote the words of a man respected by themselves, to show that the opinion I have expressed is not a hasty nor an exaggerated one. The class is, collectively, deserving of the worst I have said of them, and it is clear that I am describing them in the aggregate without detraction from the few noble and exemplary exceptions to be found in their centre.

The happiness and the well-being of the millions of Russia have been for generations in their hands. Isolated by immense distances from external pressure, supreme and absolute in the midst of their ignorant serfs, they have had a great opportunity of elevating and promoting the happiness of the latter. That they have shamefully abused that opportunity is evident to the most unreflecting traveller in their country. The power is now taken from them—the accident of birth no longer makes each among them a petty monarch. They are brought out of their retirement to the light of public observation,—and what are they? an effeminate, enervated race, in which the habits that lead to ruin are apparent; and what are the people entrusted to them and their fathers? a long oppressed and down-trodden race, who, in nine years of liberty, have shown the world already the indications of what they might have become generations since, in the hands of wise or unselfish masters.

Inseparable from the idea of a *Muscovy trader* is a vision of a bearded man in a round black cap, in a long ungraceful-looking cloth coat, and a pair of very high leather boots to meet its skirts. The modern merchant of Russia has discarded all this, and appears now-a-days on 'Change, close shaven and trim in a suit of the fashionable cut; a keen and eager man of business, liberal in his habits, large in his enterprise; a man moreover who has learned the money value of a *good position in " society."* He courts and cultivates " society," but he does so as a means and not an end. Money is his final aim and end. " Society" his means —reversing the creed of the southern sons of trade—the Frenchman whose manners he imitates, or the Englishman whose business habits he admires. He has learned thoroughly the lesson, that reputation of wealth is a sure road to its acquisition. Gorgeous furniture, sumptuous feasts, wonderful horses, and a wife hung in jewels, are his advertisements, but he has no delight in them for himself. However splendid and costly the frequent feasts he will give, " as a matter of business" to his clients, he returns with real pleasure to his peasant habits the moment that the motive for display is removed. What do such men want with money? is a natural question when one considers them.

The corporation of a country town honoured me with a dinner; and I slept at the house of a rich merchant of the place. The old gentleman took me, according to custom, into every room of his house, and showed me all the expensive property he had stuffed it with — pictures, furniture, ornaments, clocks, carpets, silver and gold—I was called on to exhaust my vocabulary of admiration. Among the rest he showed me his own bedroom, furnished with a very fine bed, and he asked me the invariable question, What did I think of that? I admired it properly—I thought it was magnificent! (it was covered with blue silk and lace.) "Yes," he said, "that cost a deal of money," but (winking as nobody but a Russian knows how to wink) "I don't sleep atop of that bed—I sleep underneath it!" The children of these merchants are in a dangerous position. As a rule, the father of the family is a man of no education, who has made his fortune too late in life to have acquired polish by the luxury of his new surroundings. There is a great gulf between himself and his children " born in the purple." He has no pleasure in their society— nor they in his. His instincts and tastes are repulsive to them, and theirs are of wasteful folly to him. He leaves them at home to the teachers and trainers he employs, whom he looks to, to direct and carry out their education. These governors and governesses too often take a pleasure in assisting nature to develope expensive and frivolous propensities, and extinguish the better instincts of their pupils. Latterly the custom has become more general of sending such children to travel through the countries of Europe. They may return more enlightened, but not often so well fitted to amass money as their parents.

The hereditary merchant or trader of the old school, who has held fast to the manners of his ancestors, is a happier, if not so great a man as his more ambitious brother. He has not made sacrifice of his domestic life, but keeps a simple home of his own, stocked with wife and children of his own rank in life, imbued with the same tastes and prejudices as himself, and sympathizing perfectly in his ruling passion for the accumulation of wealth.

Many of these old-fashioned traders are possessed of really considerable fortunes, laboriously amassed, copeck by copeck, through a long career of industry and self-denial. Considering their nationality and their love of money, it is a remarkable feature of their character, that they have subdued the Russian instinct for gambling. They do not love rash speculation in trade, nor do they play much at cards. They prefer to plod along steadily in the beaten path of their ancestors, meeting good times with additional industry, and bad times with persevering economy. They are respectable pious people, neglecting no church ordinance, and zealously observing every holiday and fast. In this as in other peculiarities they strongly resemble the Jews.

It remains to be seen whether they will bend their Russian stubbornness to compliance with the changes and innovations which the march of civilization is introducing into their country. If not, they will inevitably be crowded out of their livelihood by the upstarting of foreign and "go-a-head" competitors.

The Russian Mujik, or peasant, is a character not to be described in a few words, and the description of one type will apply to the people of the many provinces of the Empire. My own opportunities of observation have been extended to all the provinces between St. Petersburg and Siberia, and down south as far as Kief. Throughout this vast tract of territory and deep in the wilds of Siberia, the salient characteristics of the peasantry are constantly the same. It is the fashion among those who are interested in perpetuating the degradation of the Mujik, to describe him slightingly as a mere boor, without education or refinement, or the wish to acquire either; to adopt a tone of absurd condescension in intercourse with him, such as would be assumed towards a child or a superior kind of animal; and, further, to take amusement in fostering the principal vice of his character, his passion for strong drink. This was doubtless a very pretty and aristocratic amusement so long as the Mujik was tied hand and foot by the iniquitous system of serfdom, dependant for his existence on the good pleasure of a master, and without hope of achieving liberty or comfort by his own exertions. But the time is at hand when he will compete in a fair struggle for existence with his former condescending patrons, and I am no judge of character if the contest do not prove in the end that the down-trodden serf was a better man than his master.

The privileged classes and the peasantry in Russia are playing out the old fable of the two shepherd dogs, alternately spoiled by luxury in the city and invigorated by labour and hardship in the fields, and the dog best prepared to seize the wolf by the throat is still that which has the most recently led the hardest and the most laborious life.

The peasant is accused of want of education, and, to the shame of those who have held despotic control of his doings for many generations, the accusation is justified by facts. He is entirely devoid of all literary education. It is rarely indeed that a peasant is found in any of the agricultural villages who can read or write properly; and, speaking from a particular and extensive knowledge of the subject, I do not believe that one per cent. of the agricultural peasants of the centre of Russia can write their own names.

In the "Zavods" or villages collected round the great industrial undertakings, and in the Oural, and in many parts of Siberia, the percentage will be higher; but, generally, the peasant has a remarkable reluctance in confessing that he is able to write.

I have had frequent occasion to visit different villages for the purpose of making contracts for labour, charcoal, &c., with the villagers. When the terms had been agreed upon, and the contract had been drawn up, I used to call out for the "Grammaters" to come forward, and sign the contract on behalf of the community. Nobody would advance, until, having informed myself that one of them could write, I called him by name. Seeing there was no help for it, and pushed on by his companions, the talented man advanced reluctantly, and, first shaking hands with each individual—by which he was understood to acquire their power of attorney—he approached the table, and took up a pen as if it were a hot iron; and so, with intense application, after a length of time, wrote his name to the document. I have read at times that the Mujik is a careless, useless sort of animal, who does not want, or care about, education. This is not true. He does want it, and is crying out for it.

I admit that, at present, when he is so lucky as to be able to read or write, he owns to his ability with a sort of sheepish reluctance. This is only because he knows that his companions are jealous of his superior attainments, and afraid he might use them to their disadvantage.

Wherever isolated attempts have been made to remedy the really awful ignorance of the people, the schools have been intrusted to the lower orders of priests; men, as I shall show in a subsequent chapter, themselves of no education, and in other respects utterly unfitted for the charge of the schools, which in most cases were more often closed than open. I tried the experiment myself in one village, where I established a school for the children, and engaged two good teachers, first class priests, and soon had about seventy boys in constant attendance, and quite alive to the good they were doing for themselves. But I kept the school under my own supervision.

The absenteeism, or indifference of the proprietors of the land, is at the root of the evil of ignorance. These landlords, owning estates of princely extent, which they never visited, left them to the mercy of some agent, whose duties and interests ended with the collection of revenue; and if this man, as too frequently happened, were a dishonest or worthless character, the sufferings of the peasantry under his rule were terrible.

These sort of agents commonly amassed great fortunes for themselves, by a course of injustice that could only be continued so long as the peasantry remained ignorant, and consequently helpless under his extortions. It is painful, at times, to be brought into contact with the men; so timid and sheepish are they in the company of their superiors, that they seem to lose their faculties in a sort of amazement when they are spoken to.

A black-bearded son of toil was guiding me along a road,

"Well, Ivan," I said, "how many children have you?"

"Indeed, Excellency," said Ivan, "you must ask my wife; I don't know."

"What is your name?"

"Ivan."

"Yes, but your other name?"

"I have not got one; at least, I don't know it."

A messenger had been sent to me, post haste from a distant village, to inform me that some buildings were on fire.

"Well, Ivan, is it a large fire?"

"A large fire, Excellency."

"Is it a small fire, Ivan?"

"A small fire, Excellency."

"Is it very windy?"

"Very windy."

"Is it very calm weather, Ivan?"

"Very calm, Excellency." And so on.

Now, this man was, to my knowledge, no fool, but a very good charcoal-burner.

Your true Russian peasants are always remarkably cautious and polite; they habitually take off their hats to each other with the most gentlemanly gracefulness. (It may be that this practice of extreme politeness is fostered and promoted by the constant posturing of their religious observances.) But to see them at their best, one should be the guest, as I have often been, of some remote village, far from the sound of wheels, where the name of a town is hardly known; and there, while I have been waiting, perhaps for the daylight, to go bear-shooting in the woods, the members of the community (the common council of the place), hearing I was there, and having some favour to ask, or some matter of charcoal and labour to discuss, have waited upon me.

Then we would all sit round the room, and the spokesman of the party rise to explain the wishes of his community. Notice now the quiet and earnest manner of the man, the deferential bend with which he rises, the easy fluency with which he says what he has to say; how clearly and pointedly he states his facts, and how cleverly he constructs his argument; and when he has sat down again with another graceful bow, ask what sort of people they can be who describe this man as an ignorant and brutalised savage, incapable of mental and moral culture, a fit companion for a society of Calibans and Orsons.

His ignorance is not his fault. The reproach recoils on his detractors; but if his appearance, parts, and temper be those of a savage, give me savages I say, for my workmen always.

They have their own strong ideas of justice, and appreciate treatment in accordance with those ideas, as a rather amusing incident will show.

The estates I had under my management had been administered in the old manner, and the people placed under my authority had a perfect mania for sending in written documents, complaining of some real or fancied grievance, or asking for some favour. In most cases these petitions were of the most trifling, frequently absurd, description; but I made it a matter of conscience to read them all, that nothing of importance might by any chance escape my notice.

In conveying my answer to one of these petitions, my secretary told the petitioner to go to the devil. It is a place the people were very well accustomed to be sent to. Some time afterwards the man met me as I was going out. "Ah, Barrin" (this word, translated "Lord and master," was the word always used in the old times by the serf when addressing his owner), he said, "so you wished me to go to the devil. Well, I don't mind that: no doubt you know best; no doubt I shall go in time. But, you see, what we like is this: *you* read our petitions, and *then* tell us to go to the devil. Now, in the old times, when we brought a petition, they told us to go to the devil before they had read it. That is what we did not like: it was not fair."

The people would be better off if their habits were less frugal—often a few days' work will suffice to keep them in laziness for the rest of a week. Their principal food is black bread and cabbage-soup, and quass for their drink (quass is a fermentation of black bread and water). Their clothes are home-made. Each family has its own house, with its strip of the common land, generally about ten acres, more or less; its cow, horse, sheep or two; in fact, its small farm complete,—really sufficient, if properly farmed, for the support of the family, if no other resources were to be found. I have found frequently that the Russians were among the best workmen to be met with in any country. I do not mean that a Russian can do anything like the same quantity of work that an Englishman can, but he can imitate anything. Give him a model to be precisely reproduced, and he will produce it whatever it is, from a padlock to a watch. The speciality in which he excels is carpenter's work. It is commonly said that a Mujik is born with an axe in his hand. He can do wonders with this tool, and often uses no other in building and furnishing his house complete.

The worst part of the Mujik's character is his passion for vodky. In this respect are all on a level, — the otherwise most respectable members of the community and the universal ne'er-do-weels.

The Mujik does not drink constantly, nor even every day, nor every week, but on great occasions, such as a holiday or a feast, or an influx of money to his pocket, the man deliberately swallows as much vodky, and this as quickly, as he can. It is not for the sake of company that he does this. He does not give himself time to pass through a stage of elation, but he doggedly drinks off tumbler after tumbler of raw spirit, without a pause between the glasses, until at about the fifth tumbler he is perfectly drunk. Benches and tables of plain wood are provided in the "traktir," and here he sits with his head between his hands, as long as the proprietor chooses to allow,—a period measured by the amount of his custom or the demand for space for his companions in a similar condition. When the proprietor calls "time," he is escorted to the door by a waiter, who gives him a gentle push as he dismisses him in order that he may not fall on the threshold. The cold air knocks him down like a sledge hammer, and he continues his drunken slumber in the street until he is removed,—in a town by the police, in country places by his friends.

The Mujik is never, drunk or sober, a quarrelsome man. In all my experience of the country, I never remember to have seen a downright fight between two men.

They are great liars, but in a harmless way, telling insignificant falsehoods from habit more frequently than from a wish to deceive. It seems to be a part of their nature to avoid the exact truth, and to find a pleasure in the invention of plausible lies. This habit, the inevitable consequence of long subjection to tyranny, will give way to the self-respect and independence promised them under the new *régime;* for there is no vice, and generally very little motive, in a Mujik's lies. They are cunning inventors of those little plans that the thieves call " plants " in England, and, when they get into trouble, try every double and dodge to escape punishment.

I caught a number of men stealing wood and iron from my premises, and impounded their carts and horses, which I ordered to be detained until the thieves had paid twenty-five roubles each for the damage they had done. The next day these rascals had a consultation, and arranged the little comedy they were to perform for my commiseration. " Now, directly you see him," said one, "you must tumble on your knees and cry tremendously hard, and swear you have not a copeck in the world. I shall swear my wife is starving, and you will see, if we do it well, he will let us off cheap." Unfortunately for them, this little plot was arranged within my hearing; so that, when they were admitted, and had gone through the performances precisely as arranged, they found me stony-hearted as before. They persevered as long as my patience lasted, and then gave it up as of no use.

Then one of them quietly said : " If you won't let us off we must pay," and pulled out a purse full of money, and counted out the fifty roubles on the table.

" Now, Ivan," I said, " the next time that you try to humbug me, take care that I don't know all about it beforehand."

The man poked his friend in the ribs, with a laugh, and said,—" See, Maxime, the Barrin always knows what we are about."

Neither of the men was in the least disconcerted at being found out.

On that occasion I administered my own law. I was afterwards very neatly bamboozled by a peasant in collusion with the local coroner before whom I brought him.

I was passing one evening on the high road through a wood, when I heard a great shouting and scuffling among the trees.

I ran in and found one of my head foresters, a most reliable steady man, fighting with a peasant whom he had seized by the collar. Close at hand stood the cause of the battle, viz., the peasant's cart loaded with cast-iron, which the man had stolen from the works. We secured the peasant between us and brought him before the coroner, a law official appointed to make preliminary investigations in criminal cases. The coroner heard what

I and my forester had to say, and called on the prisoner to defend himself. "Oh, it is all right," said Vassily. "You see, sir, I was going through the wood along the road with my cart empty, and presently the forester called to me from out of the wood: 'Hi! Vassily Vassilivitch! come here. I have found a lot of cast iron among the trees. Just lend me your cart to take it to the works.' Of course, I did what he asked me, always being anxious to do all I can to assist the works. I took my cart into the wood and loaded the iron. Directly the iron was put into the cart—you would hardly believe it, Excellency!—the forester collared me, and said I had stolen the iron; and then the Barrin came up, and they took me away between them."

The honest and intelligent servant of the Government professed himself satisfied with this explanation: the man was discharged, and my forester and I went home looking foolish.

I was not grieved, shortly afterwards, to lose the neighbourhood of that coroner, who fell into trouble on his own account in a question of forged bank-notes, and failing to satisfy his judges on the subject, was probably sent to Siberia.

It will be perceived from the above anecdote, that scrupulous regard for the rights of property is not characteristic of the peasant class. The Mujik, in fact, is a habitual thief. But his thieving extends only so far as it is justified by his ignorance. It does not arise from any felonious intention, but from the simple reasoning of the savage, who takes what he wants and sees before him, because he is unable to understand the right of the owner who claims it. Beyond this degree there is less crime in Russia than in other countries, and the crime that exists is not relatively great among the peasantry, the faults and vices of whom all cry plainly for the remedy that will efface them—Educate!

I have often met men with small pieces of iron or wood in their hands, which they had stolen from the works. They had rather not be detected, but they are not ashamed. "Well, Ivan," I have said, "What did you steal that iron for?" "Because I wanted to make a new shovel for my wife, and this is just the piece of iron for the purpose."

As to such trifles as wood, charcoal, and the like, they say, "God has given wood, land, and water for all men alike;" and in acting up to this maxim, it is impossible to convince them that they are doing wrong.

I have said all the evil that I know of the Mujik, and I turn very willingly to pleasanter reminiscences.

Hidden away in the midst of enormous forests, scattered here and there at great distances apart, are numbers of quiet and self-sufficient little villages, whose inhabitants never wander far from the place of their birth, and scarcely know the name of the nearest town. There it is that the simplicity of the peasant character may be studied at its heart. To such a retired little village I used to go on my occasional shooting expeditions after the bear and elk, to be found in the neighbouring forests.

I always put up at the house of our Starosta, a very old man, whose wife was still active and lively at seventy years of age, and used to interest herself vastly in the conversation that passed between me and the forester, who always went with me on my hunting excursions.

This forester was a very remarkable character, who, by intelligent industry and perseverance, had raised himself from the station of a common serf, to the management of woods greater in extent than many a German principality. Moreover, he had contrived in the meantime to afford his son a liberal education, and to establish him as an artist at St. Petersburg; and, finally, by the help of those who appreciated his laudable efforts to raise his family in the social scale, he actually was enabled to enter him as a student in the academy at St. Petersburg,—an enormous promotion for the son of a serf!

The forester was a man of inquiring disposition, anxious to get information on all sorts of subjects; and our long discussions of things in general, and the world's recent history in particular, were vastly amusing, if a little perplexing to the old lady who sat and listened to them.

One morning I was smoking my pipe

before the stove, waiting for the day to break, that we might set out after a very large bear that the Starosta's son had "rung" in the neighbourhood. The forester and I were discussing the British Constitution, and I mentioned our gracious Queen, when the old lady broke into the discussion with quite a little oration. "You will excuse me," she said, "that I do not speak English. It is very funny that I cannot do it, but I cannot. I hear you always talking about your Queen Victoria; now, I want to know what does she do for our Emperor, because of course she lives at Petersburg?" "At Petersburg?" I said; "no, she lives in her own country — my country — England." "What part of Russia is England?" said the old lady. "England is not in Russia at all; it is another country by itself." But I could not convince her of that. She had never heard of any other country that was not Russia, and nothing would make her believe in its existence.

She could not get over it for a long time, and continually repeated to her husband:—" Only fancy, the Barrin trying to tell me there is another country besides Russia!"

I had a friend with me who promised to send her anything she fancied out of England. What should it be?

She asked for a handkerchief such as the peasant women wear on their heads, "only let it be a good one, silk, and plenty of colour." In due time I brought her a flame-coloured bandana from London, and told her my friend had not forgotten her wish. She admired the bright handkerchief immensely, but never could understand where it came from. I am sorry to have the following incident to relate, showing how the demons of discontent and greediness penetrated even this peaceful paradise.

The old lady had a secret grievance in her bosom—her bath-house was not fine enough; it was not even altogether weather-proof; she determined to have a new house at my expense.

One afternoon, just as the tinkling of my horses' bells must have announced my arrival to the villagers, I saw before me a lurid glare on the sky—"a house on fire in the village," I said to my forester.

"Yes," he answered, "it is the Starosta's bath-house, and there is the old witch coming out of it at this moment. Do you know what she has done? She has set fire to her bath-house for you to see it burn, and she will beg some wood of you to build a new one; and, most probably, she will ask you to give her ten times what she wants for the purpose."

Sure enough, we found the old woman crying and wringing her hands. "Oh, my bath is burned! What shall I do? What shall I do? I must live and die dirty! Oh, Barrin, give me some wood to build another house."

I told her we had been talking about her little game; but ultimately she got the wood, after making a full, free, and particular confession.

I have said the peasants have strong ideas of justice. In the olden times they looked on punishment simply as an act of tyranny and caprice on the part of their rulers; now, on the contrary, they bear no malice, but have a certain respect for a just severity.

I had occasion to send a man to the mayor of his village for gross misbehaviour, and he was condemned to receive twenty strokes with the rod.

He took the punishment patiently and went home. The next morning, however, I was told, "the Mujik who was punished yesterday wants to see you."

He had no thought of coming to revenge himself, nor even to reproach me with his punishment; but he made his bow, with a smiling countenance, and told me that, on his way home, "after I received the beating," he said, he had found tracks of a bear, which he had followed to its lair, and he wanted me to come and kill it. Now, many people would have been suspicious of such a friendly invitation to accompany to the solitudes of thick forests the man who had yesterday been flogged at their instigation; but they would have been mistaken. I went to the wood alone with this Mujik, and, after a long day's hunting, we killed the bear between us.

As I have mentioned *flogging*, it is advisable to explain the subject:—The old-fashioned "knout," with which the name of Russia has been so long in disgusting connection, is done away with; but the village community has the power to sentence one of its own members to any number of strokes, not exceeding twenty, to be given with a rod, in the presence of the mayor of the village.

That the punishment is not very severe may be concluded from the fact that this man was out with me hunting on the following day, and indeed tracked the bear on the evening of his punishment.

I believe that the sudden abolition of corporal punishment in Russia would not be understood nor appreciated by the Mujiks, who, unhappily at present, are still degraded enough to prefer flogging to fine. It must be borne in mind, that the sentence comes from the culprit's peers, and this is quite a different thing to the man's superior having power to send him to be flogged—as it was in the old *régime*.

Whenever the peasants are thrown into

contact with more civilized people, they are very quick, especially so the women, at adopting the manners and customs and dress of the latter. This is particularly to be observed in Zavod villages, where strangers come and go daily (a Zavod village is a village where a "works" is established, so called to distinguish it from the agricultural villages).

I allowed the people to walk in our park on holidays, and there I have seen women and girls dressed in white book-muslin and wearing white kid gloves.

I have written thus fully about the Mujik, with the object of giving a faithful sketch of both sides of his character, and showing him as he really is, and not as he is supposed to be. I look upon him as the one upon whom will eventually devolve the mission of developing the immense resources of his country.

In him you have the stuff of which, by

education, may be made a man of intelligence and refinement. He is neither wanting in ambition or courage. Those who have lived as I have, in the midst of the Russian peasantry, learned to know their manners, to be indulgent to their failings, to appreciate especially their " charity " and kindness of heart, will join me in raising a voice on their behalf for that education which is the one thing wanting to raise the Mujik and all Russia with him to a proper place in the world.

CHAPTER IV.

TOWNS AND VILLAGES.

THE country towns of Russia are all very much of one mould, and, with the exception of the very largest, are cheerless and miserable places. The houses are generally of wood; the streets unpaved, and badly lighted; an impassable sea of mud in wet weather, and enveloped in clouds of dust in dry.

They are only comfortable for traffic in the depth of winter, under a carpet of frozen snow.

Every Government town boasts a large

barrack-like pile of building in which are the Government offices; a great heap of stuccoed bricks and mortar, the residence of the Governor; and a few other large houses where live the rich merchants and the Tchinovnicks, who are engaged in the various offices of the State.

The rest of the better sort of houses are those of the nobility, of minor stars of the civil service; finally, of the small merchants, traders, &c., &c.

The houses in the country towns of Russia are pretty much alike.

Principally wooden constructions, the entrance hall will lead to the "saloon," the largest room in the house, with the least amount of furniture in it—a dozen and a half of chairs, a couple of card tables, a sofa couch, with a round table in front of it, a piano, always a "grand," a small carpet under the round table (the floor being parquet), two long looking-glasses mounted in nut-wood (this wood is in universal use for furniture amongst the middle classes), together with three sconces for candles—make up invariably the quantum of furniture in this the grand company room—a big picture of a saint, in the corner, and a petroleum lamp, and cigar-ash holder on the table, are the only ornaments about. This room leads to what we should call the drawing-room, of much smaller proportions, and a little more showily fitted up; minus the piano, the individual pieces of furniture will be about the same. This drawing-room leads to the sleeping apartment of the master and mistress, and if the owners are of a particularly religious turn of mind, this room will be noticeable from the collection of pictured images in the corner, many of them liberally adorned with precious stones, diamonds and emeralds being the favourites. The other peculiarities of this room will be the smallness of the bed, in which the fortunate possessors snooze away a large proportion of their day, and the absence of what we should call the common necessary of a good washstand. The idea in this way being, a boil on Saturday night in the bath, and a sort of sensation of a "dry wipe" on the other six days of the week. Russians are always astonished at what they consider the immoderate consumption of water by Britons, and a Russian servant will be a long time understanding why one requires anything more for his morning ablutions than the tiniest brass basin and pint pot of water, which he has been accustomed to serve for the use of his native master. I travelled for a long time with a great man, whose servant every morning presented him with a small silver pie-dish-looking basin and its accompaniment of a half pint silver mug of water, and this was all the wash he gave himself for a fortnight.

To return to the house, the dining-room is peculiar in the respect of having no furniture in it but what is absolutely necessary, namely, dining-table, chairs, buffet, and a side-table or two, and is never used for other purposes than those of eating. A few other bedrooms are stowed away out of sight. The kitchen is generally outside the house in the yard, and the servants sleep where they can. The houses are well built, with thick walls, and good roofs.

Many towns have also their small theatre, their nobility club, generally supplemented by a merchants' club, a hotel or two, several fire towers, the indispensable "Gostini or Dwor," or bazaar, of very oriental character, where every kind of merchandize is exposed, from lucifer matches to diamonds; in the streets a few independent shops, away from the bazaar; an extraordinary number of churches, disproportionate to the population, whitewashed and gaily painted on the exterior with figures of their patron saints, and generally a couple of monasteries, and always dotted here and there miserable sheds or huts, where the Butoschniks or Russian police live.

The theatre generally depends for its performances on the arrival of some company of strolling actors, who pass their lives travelling from town to town, making a short stay at each. Their acting is superior to that we are accustomed to expect under such conditions. The Russians are all very fond of the stage and are generally by no means contemptible actors.

They have also for the most part a very good taste for music, and most of the towns are provided with a band, which performs very creditably.

The club is generally opened only three times a week, excepting in the largest towns, where it is opened every day.

Its principal use is for gambling; at certain intervals balls and bal-masqués are given. The bal-masqué does not deserve its name. It is a sort of *converzatione*, at which the ladies only wear black masks and dominoes; the gentlemen in evening dress or uniform, without masks, walk about with them; the band plays music, but nobody dances at all.

The institution in my opinion is a dreary failure, amusing enough perhaps among the livelier nations of the South, but solemnly performed by an assembly of stolid semi-civilized Russians, its close resemblance to a funeral party is appalling.

The hotels are generally detestably dirty and uncomfortable, swarming with bugs; but they are improving of late, and now, in some towns, as Nijny Novgorod, Kazan, and others of that class, they are clean and comfortable, boasting of French cookery and good clean beds.

It is a rash proceeding, however, to put up at a country town of the ordinary sort, unless you bring with you the materials for your own beds, without which no Russian of the better sort thinks of setting out on his travels.

I was travelling about two years ago in the south-central provinces, and after a night passed on the road, was glad to arrive at Tambov about five in the morning, and looked forward to a few hours sleep at the hotel of that town.

One of the grandees of the province, a great proprietor, had passed me on the road, and kindly undertaken to order that a room should be ready for my arrival. We drew up at the door of the hotel, which was ornamented with a board inscribed "Tabell Dot," and I followed the waiter to my bed-room. At my first glance at that miserable apartment, I understood how illusory had been the hopes that I had indulged of refreshment and rest. All the furniture of the room was a table, three chairs, a looking-glass—that must have been used as a target for some heavy projectile—and a sofa of moth-eaten and dusty rusty appearance, insufficiently stuffed and cushioned, and rickety in all its joints. Bed and bedding were not: and I planned to contrive with my railway rugs, if the waiter would find me a sheet. Nothing more simple; he would fetch me a sheet immediately. He was a long time doing so, and in the end brought me a dirty table-cloth. Deciding to forego the luxury of sheets, I found that I must at least have a pillow — that article of furniture which every Russian carries about with him wherever he goes. A pillow was promised immediately, away went the waiter to fetch it. This time he was longer than before, and returned with a bundle made up in a napkin, which finally dispelled my wish to try to sleep on the rickety sofa.

The Russian prince in the next room, who had a whole baggage waggon full of his own conveniences, was comfortable enough, and found no fault with the accommodation of the hotel. In the country Traktirs or inns in Russia you are always told you can have anything you wish to eat or drink. I went to dine at a Traktir in a small town on the Oka. The waiter came to take my orders, and this was what we said—

I. "Well, Ivan, what have you got?"

Waiter. "Anything that your excellency chooses to order."

I. "Fresh salmon, for instance?"

W. "Certainly, excellency."

Now fresh salmon were never brought within three hundred miles of this place.

I. "Well, bring me some fresh salmon and cucumber."

W. "Sichas!" (This is the Russian "*Yessir*." The words mean "this hour," it is what the waiters always say. I have determined its real meaning to be, "Don't you wish you may get it?")

In three minutes my waiter came back from the kitchen with, "Very sorry, sir; but the cook has just served up the last of the salmon."

I. "Well, Ivan, what have you now?"

W. "Anything you choose."

I. "Then bring me roast mutton."

W. "Sichas!"

Another visit to the kitchen, and in a short delay, another report, "Cook is very sorry, but unfortunately he has got no mutton to-day."

I. "Then tell me at once what you have."

W. "Unfortunately, nothing but eggs to-day."

Finally, he cooks me the eggs in my presence—the kitchen fire and the cook being as purely the creation of his imagination as the salmon and cucumbers and Barmecide roast mutton.

The monotony of life in the towns offers nothing of interest to describe. It includes much eating and drinking, a great consumption of champagne in the richer towns, and perpetual card playing. It is varied at intervals by a performance at the theatre, and the ball of the season at the club. In a few of the large towns, where more of the higher sort of government officers are stationed, and the best of the nobility live, the time can be passed agreeably enough.

Every town of any importance has its

prison. I believe these buildings are greatly improved in late years.

Passing through Vladimir, the capital town of the government of that name, I called in to see the prison, and visited every room. They have the custom of keeping prisoners for minor crimes in large wards, the sleeping accommodation being reclining boards, fitted up in rows, in the same room the day is spent in. These prisoners seemed rather "jolly" than otherwise. Those criminals accused of graver offences were confined, generally two or three together, in cells in other parts of the building. I only saw one man shut up by himself, and he had murdered two people; this fellow was described as "secret," not at all implying, as many have supposed, a political prisoner, but the term is used for the worst sort of criminals relative to the treatment they receive in prison.

I noticed in this gaol a nobleman, locked up for a sufficiently grave offence, who was in ordinary costume; and I was informed that it was his "nobility" that gave him the privilege of dispensing with the prison dress.

The women's wards were on a separate side, and the superintendent told me he found it very difficult to keep their side as clean as that of the men.

The kitchen was well kept (all prison labour), and the food was good. Certainly Vladimir prison gives one a favourable idea of its management and of its superintendent.

The country villages in the north and centre of Russia are invariably cheerless and ugly collections of grim timber boxes, called houses, built entirely of wood, roofs and all, without a bit of thatch, or a patch of green, or a flower, or spot of colour of any kind to enliven the sepia dulness of the place. The interior of these wooden houses is arranged with a regard to the extreme vicissitudes of the climate; the part of the house which, in summer, is the dwelling-room of the family, is abandoned when the cold weather sets in, and they retreat to the neighbourhood of the great stove, used in the warm season as a kitchen; near the top of the stove are their sleeping berths, suspended at a distance of about eighteen inches from the ceiling. Here the little children climb up to roost, while the parents and older members of the family make their beds on the top of the stove itself. The only furniture to be seen in these miserable homes is a table, and a large wooden bench fixed round the walls of the apartment; a few pictures of the saints hanging in the corners and invariably a large showy trunk, painted in many colours, and bound round and round with iron hoops. This trunk contains all the treasures that belong to the family; a dress or two, brought to the daylight on festive occasions, heir-looms it may be of the mother; a few towels, which are always handsomely trimmed with lace, by which also the peasants set great store, and with respect to which they observe the following curious custom at their weddings:—

The bride and bridegroom, coming to pay their respects to the Barrin, the bride hands him such a towel on a plate, which he accepts; and, in return, lays on the same plate a pocket-handkerchief, with some roubles in the folds.

Besides the drapery and towels, the big chest may contain a loaf or two of cake bread, a few groceries, and other small articles.

A small corner near the stove is partitioned off for cooking, and provided with the necessary utensils.

Small and large insects increase and multiply in the warmth and dirt of the wooden huts. The people are superstitious about a kind of cockroach, called in Russia "tarakan," which are held to bring good luck with their company.

The children of the peasantry run about wild, and free from correction or training, but are always well treated by their parents. In fact, I believe that no people can be fonder of their children than the Russian peasants are.

They are all strong and healthy; like the young Spartans, the hardship of their lives kills all the weakly ones. Hence the whole race is healthy and sound, and by the severity of their "struggle for existence," improving in every generation. In the depth of winter the children are hardened or killed;

one moment in the biting air, the next in the stifling room. A medical doctor, who has had much experience among the Mujiks, told me that from statistics he had carefully collected, he found that *two-thirds* of the children of the peasantry die before they are a twelvemonth old. A bath is attached to every house, in which all the members of the family are boiled regularly every Saturday. On the other days of the week they do not use water for washing, except in compliance with their very oriental prejudice, to wash their hands before eating. They all sleep in a portion of the clothes they wear by day, which they never take off, except for the Saturday bath.

In all their doings they are the bond-slaves of precedent and routine (another striking characteristic that they have in common with the Asiatic nations). Thus, on a certain day in the year, which is a holiday, generally called among them "Apple-day," the priests pronounce a solemn benediction on their ripening fruit; then, and only then, will the people begin to eat apples; nothing will induce them to do so before, as they believe that if they do they will get the cholera. In the towns as well as in the country this rule is observed; and when the day for oranges has come, they will on no account eat any more apples, and you will find it hard to get one anywhere. So, in the villages, they have a fixed day in the year when they begin all at one time the practice of bathing in the lakes and rivers, and another fixed day when they leave it off. I once saw a great quantity of wild fowl, as I was being ferried across a river by a sporting boatman, and I asked him when the young ducks would be ready to shoot. He named the day; of course, one of their holidays; and although he might be tempted by any number of "flappers" long before the time, he would not think of shooting them until the appointed day arrived.

Among the practices with which the people welcome Easter, the old Christian custom of greeting one another on that festival with a kiss, is carried to an intolerable extent, and has lost all meaning. For a week beforehand they are all busy boiling and painting eggs, which they are to present to each other with a kiss. Immediately the clock strikes twelve, the privilege or penance, as the case may be, commences. Nobody then considers himself insulted by the combined offer of a kiss and an egg. In a few cases it may be confessed that the trouble is a pleasure; but when it comes, as it did with me, to a long line of several hundred workmen (mostly engaged in charcoal burning, in the stoking and poking of fires and chimneys, and other deeds of darkness), the poetical and sentimental point of view of the religious custom is completely shut out and supplanted by the intolerable annoyance.

One may talk of the Balaklava charge, the storming of the Redan, and such exploits; think of the nerve that was required to stand my ground before a bearded and vodky-loving Mujik, with cinders in his beard, and charcoal-dust in the pores of his skin— a man who had been breaking calcined ore, perhaps, all night, and looking like the doubtful progeny of an African negro or a red Indian in his war-paint. Think of my horror of suspense while one after the other, a whole regiment of such smutty objects, shuffled up to my place, each drawing a dusty sleeve across his sooty mouth, each diving to the bottom of his pocket for the painted egg, prepared carefully for this occasion, each taking off his hat and calling me down to the punishment with the politest of bows—the most respectful of grins; and when the first hundred had kissed me three hundred times in the aggregate, to know that another hundred had to come after them. Here were courage and endurance worthy of a greater cause. But I should have done wrong to avoid the courtesy, and very likely deeply offended the people, to whom it was often the expression of a long-cherished feeling of gratitude for favours which I perhaps knew nothing of, or had forgotten long since.

There are no people who more cordially appreciate the sympathy of their superiors with their own festive and religious usages than the Russian peasants.

Russia has long been known as the country of bells, and these are heard with a vengeance when they are sounded to usher in Easter-day. Exactly at midnight, with the last toll of the clock, a gun is fired, and, at once every belfry peals forth loudly and merrily in a chorus that shakes the air.

After a time the official ringers are tired and give place to volunteers, and the belfries are crowded with boys, who ring incessantly throughout the day, deafening the neighbourhood.

CHAPTER V.

PRIESTS, CHURCH, AND EMPEROR.

THE reverence which the Russians, particularly the lower classes, have for their religion is remarkable, but it is only to their religion itself that their respect extends, by no means to the priests, its ministers.

In Russia you will never see a village of the slightest importance, that has not its church, and many have two or three. It is often a striking thing to see a miserably poor and small village overshadowed by an enormous church almost large enough to contain the whole village in itself.

The churches are always built by the landowners. They are much finer and more plentiful in the centre of Russia than in the north. The services are numerous, and for these and the innumerable church holidays and their vigils, the bells are perpetually in motion. Fortunately the bells are always of a very fine tone, and produce an effect very different to the tinkling or dismal metallic clang of the bells of some of our country churches in England. The interiors of the churches are all made gorgeous by silver and gold, which give a brilliant reflection to hundreds of candles during service; and pictures of the saints in handsome frames hang from the walls and columns. The Greek Church admits no graven images within her sanctuaries. The church is generally lighted with a great number of candles burning on heavy ornamental candlesticks of different sizes.

Musical instruments are forbidden by the orthodox discipline, but the choir of male voices is generally decidedly good, and fills the building with a volume of sound, more effective and more solemn even than the tones of an organ. The congregation do not take part in the singing, which is entirely performed by persons attached to the church.

In the robes of the priests and in the whole arrangement of the accessories to worship, there is a display of barbaric splendour, that doubtless finds its response in the nature of the semi-civilized people whom it is designed to dazzle and attract.

The blessing of the Church is invoked on every circumstance of Russian life.

Moving into a new house, building an engine, laying the foundation of a factory, or starting a locomotive; finally, all special occasions of change, or of beginning anything, are incomplete and unlucky, unless they are made propitious by the spoken blessing of the Church.

Every room in every house, whether it be your own private dwelling-room, or public shop, or, that scene of debauchery, the village "traktir," contains the likeness of a saint, who must be blind and deaf indeed, or lead a horrid life of mental torture, one would think, in presiding over the bacchanalian proceedings of the vodky store. Every orthodox Russian, as an indispensable companion on a journey, puts his saintly picture in his pocket before he sets out. He would as soon leave his hat behind him as his patron saint.

In his infancy a cross or image is hung round his neck, which from that time to the day of his death, never leaves him under any circumstances, and is never taken off for any purpose. I have said that although the people have a deep reverence for their religion, they have little or no respect for their priests. It is fortunate for the country and themselves that this is so, for if such a superstitious people had the same blind faith in their priests that they have in the outer ceremonies of their Church, then the destinies of the country would be in the hands of as worthless, ignorant, and immoral a set of hypocrites as the world contains.

There are two distinct orders of priests, widely separted in character and position.

The upper class, the hierarchy or aristocracy of the priesthood, from among whom all the higher dignitaries of the Church are appointed, are called the Black Clergy. These are an educated body of men.

The lower order, who are shut out from the loaves and fishes, and condemned never to rise above the rank of a parish priest, are by far the most numerous, and in general the only clergy to be found away from the capitals or towns and monasteries. Their office is hereditary from father to son, and they are not admitted to a cure until they are married, but are forbidden to contract a second marriage if their first wife dies. The monastic order adopt celibacy as their rule. The village priests are a wretched, drunken, immoral, altogether disreputable class. On the great holidays of the Church, they are as frequently drunk as any of their parishioners, indeed, very often the priest sets the first example of drunkenness. This is not to be wondered at, as they are accustomed, on such occasions, to make the tour of their village, calling at every house to consecrate anew the images and leave their benediction with the family, for which they receive, in each house, a small sum of money and a glass of spirits.

If their self-respect were to prompt them

to discontinue this custom so degrading to their sacred office, they might starve, as it is by such means that they collect the principal part of their living. They have hardly any fixed income, no tithes or claim to settled contributions, but depend upon what they collect among their, frequently, poverty-stricken parishioners.

Even the collecting-boxes placed in the churches, to which every devout worshipper will habitually contribute a few copecks from time to time, are not exclusively for the good of the priests, but applied to support the church itself; and the most devout of their flock give very grudgingly a few copecks to their unfortunate priests, however liberal they may be to the church.

The opportunity of a great festival is therefore not to be neglected by a needy priest going round to sanctify the images; and on the principle of his church, to require payment for every sacerdotal function, and so collect a few roubles for his needs.

The peasant is glad of the occasion to renew the sanctity of his penates (somewhat scandalised, as these last may be supposed to be by the indulgences that they have witnessed), and welcomes the priest with the irrepressible hospitality of his nation, and offers him something to eat and drink. A priest fond of good living on a special festival — Easter for instance, must be unusually strong in the head, if he can hold out against the repetition of the slight refection and spirits that he takes at all the houses of his village.

The priest is also a welcome guest at all family festivities, such as a marriage feast, or a funeral dinner. Every funeral ends with a dinner, and the more jolly and convivial the guests, the greater honour to the departed friend.

With all their faults, drunk or sober, the priests never allow the appointed services of their church to be neglected. There are nearly always, at least, two priests to every church, so that in the event of the incapacity of one, the other may act; and I never heard of an instance when the Church service was not punctually performed.

I believe that the fees appointed for the ministrations of the Church, for marriages, burials, &c., are very small, and a great deal of bargaining takes place on the occasion of a burial; the peasant's mind being then divided between his desire to release his departed friend from purgatory by a liberal expenditure, and his mistrust of the price the priest sets on the necessary masses.

The Russians are very liberal in this matter, and will strip themselves to their last copeck, to secure the offices of the Church on behalf of their dead. I have again and again been applied to by peasants for the loan of a few roubles, when they could not raise a sufficient sum to meet the demands of the priest in such a case.

The priests are assisted in the services of the Church by one or two deacons and sacristans, who intone parts of the service, and are generally selected on account of their fine bass voices. The sacristans are commonly without education, and sometimes unable to read, but they know the services by heart, and may be seen turning over the leaves of the book before them, and feigning to read the prayers that they chant, while the book is upside down. The service is not performed in the modern Russian language, but in the old Sclavonic. The congregation are not expected to be able to follow the service verbally, but have a general idea of the meaning of its different parts. The churches contain no seats, and the chosen attitude for prayer is erect, with the head bowed. The prayers are accompanied with the incessant act of making the sign of the Cross on the face and chest.

The litany is solemn and impressive, but contains the most extraordinary number of repetitions of one phrase, so that the priest, for instance, will continue for a quarter of an hour repeating as rapidly as his tongue can form the sounds, such a phrase as " Gospodi pomcelui." *

The marriage ceremony has been frequently described. At its conclusion, after the priest has declared the couple before him to be man and wife, he takes in his own the hands of bride and bridegroom, and, walking backwards, leads them three times round the church, in the face of the congregation. This is the most solemn and

---

* God have mercy upon us.

impressive feature of their wedding customs. The rest have, more or less, a smack of barbarism. The custom, for example, of payment by the woman, or her parents, to induce the man to marry her, has no resemblance to anything like dowry. The husband is always (as it were) the "stalled ox" of the family, privileged to frequent spells of drunken rest; while the wife labours always, and usually does more than the man for the support of the household.

For this convenience every peasant, as soon as he arrives at marriageable years, looks out for himself a strong, hearty, young wife, an efficient beast of burden. These are not scarce in a Russian village, the young people are generally strong and healthy; the feeble ones dying in their infancy. When he has found the young woman, the next question is, what will she give for the privilege of becoming his household drudge, or what will her parents give to be rid of her. He fixes a sum that he considers adequate to compensate him for the surrender of all his charms to one young person; and lets her parents know that if they will pay him so much, he will marry their child. For the lowest class of peasants, the terms are generally about twenty roubles a man, and a new suit of cloth clothes, and a certain number (settled by treaty) of cotton shirts, a hat, pair of boots; in fact, a complete equipment. The bride must also bring her own trousseau, every article of which is settled between contracting parties before the wedding goes forward. The extent to which the man is clothed at the expense of his bride, is apparently in proportion to the rank of the parties.

In the lowest ranks, as I have said, a complete equipment is required; but in the highest classes the custom is observed by the provision of a warm dressing-gown for the gentleman, which is afterwards replaced as it wears out from the wife's private resources. The daughter of the chief shopkeeper of our village, when she married the foreman of the other shop, gave him, I know, among other things, six dozen shirts.

When all financial preliminaries are satisfactorily adjusted, the marriage of the peasants proceeds, still at the cost of the bride and her relations, who invite the bridegroom and his friends to meet, at a succession of family feasts, her own female friends. Thus rewarding these last for any help they may have given in making the bridegroom's breeches and shirts, by affording them an opportunity of picking up husbands for themselves. At these entertainments the principal amusements are dancing and playing at a game resembling that which, in England, is called "Kiss in the ring."

At the wedding they provide a great box bound in every direction with iron hoops, and gaudily painted; in this the bride-offering of apparel for self and husband is carefully packed, and carried about with them through the whole of the day's proceedings; first to the church, and afterwards to the traktir, to which they adjourn from the religious service, and at which they consume, in drinking, a great part of the dowry of the bride, until they sally forth intoxicated, and with cat's music of castanets and saucepans, parade the streets of the place with their friends, disguised in ridiculous costumes—a miserable sight for all those who appreciate the latent good qualities of their character.

Their bacchanalian diversions are repeated for two or three days, probably until they have spent the dowry and the amount of the gifts of their friends; when, at last, the big box finds rest in its permanent home, and the bride begins to settle down to serious work. Altogether, a peasant's wedding can only be regarded in the light of a nuisance, and the sooner their practices on such occasions are modified or changed altogether the better for the people.

Even the better sort of peasantry, who do not hold their feasts in a traktir, but at home, and who also refrain from parading the streets in their folly, dine and dance at the house of the bride's father for twenty-four hours unceasingly, assisted and kept in countenance by the deacons of the church, who distinguish themselves as well by their agility as by their appetites.

All persons present at funerals carry each a lighted taper in his hand.

Hired mourners are invariably employed on the occasion of a death, and watch the body alternately for three days and two nights, which are allowed to elapse between death and burial. The coffin is never nailed down until the time when it is actually deposited in the grave, and each of the mourners kisses the forehead of the corpse the moment before it is enclosed. In the summer time this practice is obviously unhealthy and disagreeable, and the smell of the corpse is hardly counteracted by abundant censing of the church.

They use interesting and peculiar ceremonies, of whose meaning and origin I regret that I can give no account, at the consecration of the altars in new churches. In the first place, a clean wooden table, as white as snow, is brought in, and a nail is driven into each of its four corners; then the priests all put on large white aprons, and go through the ceremony of washing the table, first with soap and water, and then with red wine; the heads of the four nails are then covered with wax, and the table is anointed with scented oil, a strong perfume, and finally covered with a snow-white linen cloth, and over this a splendidly embroidered altar cloth is laid. The congregation in the meantime stand round, bearing each a lighted taper, and crowd to the table to secure fragments of the wax with which the heads of the nails are covered, or to moisten their handkerchiefs with the scented oil of anointment; if they succeed in either case, they rejoice in the belief that they possess in the relic an infallible preventive of pain or disease.

I have alluded only slightly to the one or two ceremonies of the church which I accidentally fell in the way of witnessing. Naturally, they are not of a class to come frequently under my notice, and I believe there are ceremonies which I have not seen still more interesting and peculiar than those I have tried to describe as I saw them.

A great addition is made to the priests'

revenues by the custom of processions of the very holy images of their churches. At Moscow, for example, there is an image of the Virgin Mary, which is provided with a carriage and four horses, and makes a daily round of visits among the faithful of the congregation. So great is the desire of the people to receive this holy image into their houses, that application is made several months in advance for the privilege.

When it passes along the streets, its attendants bareheaded, it is the universal practice for everybody within sight to uncover in reverence for it. In the country it is the custom for these images to make annually a tour through their neighbourhood. The one that passed through our village every year came from a distant monastery, and, on its arrival, was taken first to the church, where a religious ceremony was performed in its presence; after which, it was carried from house to house, and the priests collected fees at every visit. To give it house-room for the night was, however, the greatest honour, bought by a considerable fee. The amount collected upon these excursions is astonishing.

I heard that in our village the offerings amounted in ten days to about 4,000 s. r., say, £500, more or less.

The procession starts from its shrine with no other companions than a few priests and women, and, perhaps, an imbecile man or two; and, in every village, all the beggars and imbeciles attach themselves to it, until a great crowd of ragged and pitiable people is formed—undesirable guests in any house. They all crowded into my house once a year, and when they left, the windows were necessarily thrown open, and strong scents burned in the rooms where they had passed.

The number of the saints was steadily

increasing in all parts of Russia to so unreasonable an extent, that the present Emperor found it necessary to issue a ukase, which forbad that any more were placed in the calendar.

It is not uncommon to meet men who think and insist that the saints have visibly appeared to them. I am inclined to attempt to account for the superstition in the following way :—

Russia is a country where one continually sees mirage. I was driving once over a part of Russia—not exactly steppe country, but among extensive plains—when my companion and I saw a man in the fields. He was standing still, but had a peculiar look about him. I cannot describe what this look was; but although he was unmistakably a man, he did not look exactly earthly.

So much was I struck with this singularity of his appearance, that I kept my eyes on him. I supposed I watched him thus for about half a minute, when he gradually disappeared. No doubt this vision was an optical delusion, caused by mirage. When I questioned my coachman about it, he appeared to be somewhat frightened, and began at once to say we had seen a saint. I have no doubt a great many Russian saints can be accounted for by a similar explanation, and the following story bears out my opinion in that respect :—

The same coachman was driving me along a road, about ten versts distant from a certain provincial town in the government of Vladimir, where there is a small chapel, which I had often noticed.

"What is that chapel for?" I asked the coachman.

"That is Elias's chapel," he replied. "One day some people who were coming out of town saw a saint on the road, and tried to catch him; but he disappeared. A few days afterwards they saw him again, and tried to catch him, but he again disappeared; soon afterwards he appeared for the third time, and again disappointed his pursuers by vanishing in a small pool of water that was there. Hereupon the faithful at once subscribed and built this chapel over the spot, and the anniversary of his appearance is kept as a great holiday, and the water in the pool has great healing powers on those occasions."

I asked how long ago these appearances happened? "About forty years," was the answer. No doubt this was a mirage saint.

A priest or deacon, who had charge of the chapel, lived in a small hut near, and I had often noticed, across the road opposite his house, a sort of wooden bird-trap fixed on a post, about four feet from the ground, just the sort of trap that boys make of bricks to catch birds. I could not imagine what this was for. One day, when the sound of my bells must have just reached him, I saw the old man pop out of his house and go to the trap; as I passed the trap, I saw he had put a small cucumber in. I rattled by, and turned my head again to see what this could mean, when I saw the old priest run out again, cross the road to the trap, and take out his cucumber with an air of the greatest disappointment. Then it dawned upon me what the trap was for. The old man, finding I never contributed to the empty trap, *baited it*, when he heard me coming, with the cucumber. I was sorry not to have understood the poor old gentleman before, but afterwards I began to throw in a small donation to the box as I passed.

Looking out of my window one morning, I was astonished by the spectacle of three suns, all of the same brilliance, so that I could not distinguish the parhelia from the real orb. But this phenomenon is not common, excepting in the extreme northern parts of the Empire.

Great as is the reverence of the Russian people for their Church, it does not surpass that which they have for their Emperor.

The love of a Russian peasant for his Czar is an indescribable sentiment. The Czar is to him an incarnation of Providence on earth—an almost omniscient and perfect being—created for the special protection of the peasantry, responsible for nothing that goes wrong, but the source of every alleviation that smooths the Mujik's rough road of life. The peasants are perfectly childish in this affection, with which no little superstition is mixed, so that prayers to the saints are not seldom mingled with his majesty's name, not only as the subject but as the object also of their prayers. They believe that the Emperor knows each one of them personally, and takes a fatherly interest in the welfare of every individual.

I remember once going into a village and saying to a very old woman, the mother of the village :—

"Well, old lady, I have been to Nijny Novgorod, and shown the Czarevitch some of our iron."

"Ah," she said, "did he think it was good?"

"Yes; he thought it was very good."

"He knew it was made with our charcoal, I suppose?" That meant the charcoal burned by her husband and others.

"Of course," I said.

"Did he ask after my husband?"

Not to spoil what I thought was a happy illusion for the old woman, I nodded yes.

"Ah, yes," she soliloquized, "of course

the Czarevitch knew that my husband is the foreman of the charcoal burnings."

It struck me that there was something very significant in that notion, of the intimate hold that the Emperor and his family have on the hearts and minds of the peasantry.

But they have the most curious ideas on this subject. They think, one and all, that they have only to go to St. Petersburg, and knock at the door of the palace, to gain immediate access to the Czar, and a hearing of any petition they want to lay before him.

More than once, for example, when I have had some dispute with workmen, I could not agree to their demands, or they were asking for some absurdity, they would say:—

"Never mind, we will go to the Emperor, and tell him, and he will soon make you do what we want."

And, in fact, I have known more than

once, a deputation actually to start off on their mission " to the Emperor," with some absurd grievance for him to set right, and only to return because stopped on the road by some official person whom they trusted, who would convince them of the absurdity of their demands: not of their project of "appealing to Cæsar."

I knew a very respectable Mujik, who was at one time a rich man for his class, but who, in an unlucky hour, had discovered somewhere a deposit of iron pyrites, and, deceived by the silver-gilt glitter of this mineral, he concluded at once that it was silver or gold, and his fortune was made. He had wasted all his property in having his treasure constantly watched for a long time, when, at last, he came to me one day, with a small bag full of his pyrites in his hand.

After he had carefully secured the door, he looked all about the room and under the table, to make sure there were no listeners within hearing, and then produced his minerals :—

"What's that?" said he.

"Sulphur and iron," I answered.

"Not a bit of it! That is silver."

I put a piece on the fire, and all the sulphur burned out of it, and showed him there was no silver in the residue; but it had no effect on his conviction that the pyrites was silver.

"No;" he said. "I see you don't understand it. You have never seen our silver ore here; but I am going off to see the Emperor, to show him my silver. Unfortunately, I am short of money; will you lend me five roubles, to eat on my way?"

I had a liking for the man, and, after telling him he was a fool, gave him the five roubles, and away he went, to walk to the Emperor.

Several weeks after this I was driving through our village, when I saw somebody running after me, calling out to stop. I stopped, and picked up my old friend the treasure-seeker, returning sobered from his travels.

"Well, Feodor," I said, "did you see the Czar?"

"Oh, no,—it was all a mistake. When I got to Moscow, I saw my General (the peasant did not belong to us), and he took me to a clever man, who said it was just the same that you told me; so I came home again. I only spent two roubles thirty copecks of your money, and here is the change," which he gave me. "I have not done so badly, after all," he said; "whilst I was away, all the Mujiks were certain it was silver, and my wife has sold them all I had, at three roubles a pound!"

The Russian peasants may well carry their

love for their Czar to excess, and believe the man who has done so much for them to be something higher and holier than a fellow human being. These thirty millions of slaves whose chains he suddenly broke, have been *told that he did so;* and they, better than all the world, know and appreciate the enormous amount of opposition he must have conquered in the nobles before he could do it, as well as the enormous value of the boon he has conferred on themselves by his victory. For I assert the final liberation of the serfs of Russia to be the greatest and noblest victory over prejudice and tyranny that the will of one man ever won.

The liberated serfs are intoxicated with their liberties, and their ideas on the subject are very curious. They believe,—as a Mujik told me,—" You see Barrin, things are altered now. There was a time when I and everything that belonged to me was yours; but now you, and everything that belongs to you, is *mine.*"

It is infinitely more healthy for the ignorant people to hold that opinion, absurd as it is, than to be in the abject state they were before. It is better to be offended by the outspoken bearing of free men than disgusted by the falsehood of servility. I overheard two Mujiks talking under my balcony about myself.

"Ivan, who is that chap up there?"

"Oh! he is one of those German fellows (all foreigners are called Germans) who have rented the works."

No *serf* would have dared take the measure of his master—German or Russian—like that. But the significance of the anecdote will be lost upon those who have not known Russia and the peasants under the old *régime.* I am horrified when I read, as I do sometimes, that the emancipation is a failure. Let those who take interest in the question whether millions of men should be slaves or free, go to Russia and judge for themselves. Let them go into the villages and talk with the people—hear what they have to say on their own behalf; and then, even in ignorance of their misery under their former condition, I am sure they cannot doubt that the Russian peasant deserves, and is capable of using to good purpose, the rights and advantages of liberty.

CHAPTER VI.

SPORTS AND PASTIME.

THERE is no country within the same distance from our own which affords such excellent sport as Russia; but the Russians are not a sporting people; they understand nothing beyond pot-hunting, and their neglect of the game is perhaps a reason why there is more for other people.

In Russia we have every kind of game known in England, and a great deal more besides; but pheasants are only found in the Caucasus. Generally all over Russia, are to be found partridges (grey and Frenchmen), black game, capercailzie, rabchick or tree partridges, ptarmigan, snipe of all sorts, hares, ducks, geese, swans, woodcock, and all other kinds of wild fowl, and bustards in the steppes.

Among the larger game are bears, elk, wolves, and lynxes, and in the Oural roedeer. In the neighbourhood of the Altai mountain range, tigers have been shot, and some stuffed specimens are preserved in the museum at Barnaoul.

These had no doubt found their way across the Kirghis Steppe; and so wandered to the Altai provinces, to the south of Semipalatinsk.

A good many owls of the large horned sort, perfect monsters to look at, have been found in the Oural mountains.

In the government of Nijny Novgorod, and parts of Vladimir, I have seen innumerable eagles of all sorts and colours, and among them buzzards or fish eagles. Some of the large black eagles I have seen were wonderful to behold. I have a special recollection of one very large one which I saw on a tree, I unluckily had not my gun with me. I made demonstrations to frighten him off, which he did not notice for a long time; and, when he did condescend to pay attention to my shouting and projectiles, he looked so remarkably as if he was preparing to make a swoop in my direction, that he ended by *frightening* me off.

All the small game in those parts have so little knowledge by experience of guns and men, that they are as tame as Selkirk's subjects, and one literally treads on the birds; and has to kick them up to be shot at, like the pheasants in a good preserve at home.

The bustards come on to the corn land

about the steppes after harvest. These birds are particularly partial to peas. They are very large, sometimes weighing up to 35 lb., and are hard to get at in these steppes where there is no cover of any sort, and the only way to get a shot is to be covered up in a cart-load of hay, drive as near as possible to the birds, and wait patiently for a long shot with a pea-rifle.

These birds are sometimes miscalled wild turkeys, but they have very little of the turkey about them. They are not bad eating, if you bury them twenty-four hours in the earth before you cook them.

The Siberian animals, which are hunted for their fur, as the sable, lynx, ermine, and others, were, doubtless, at one time common in Russia too; and, as to beaver, I once came across a very curious document relating to them.

It was a privilege granted by Ivan the

Terrible, who reigned about 1560, to certain peasants of a village in the present government of Vladimir, to hunt and take beavers in the neighbouring woods. The document was doubtless genuine, and the country it named was that which Ivan passed through — then a dense forest, unexplored, and scarcely passable—on his way to the siege and capture of Kazan. The permission was said to be given to the peasants to reward them for guiding Ivan and his army through the woods; which for ages afterwards were known by the name of Mourom Woods; and which to this day, although all cleared away and cultivated, are mixed up in all legends and rhymes as the dreaded haunts of robbers and wild beasts.

Very few among the peasants shoot, but here and there one is met with who is a sportsman; and when that is the case, he is always a thoroughly good one. In the

Oural, where shooting is rather more general, the peasants always use an immensely heavy pea-rifle, with which they shoot all kinds of game.

There are game laws, and a close time fixed, but very little attention is paid to either, excepting in the neighbourhood of large towns.

Generally, when a peasant in the country is out with his gun, he shoots whatever he gets a chance at; that is to say, anything sitting—he will very seldom risk wasting his ammunition on a flying shot.

Almost every kind of shooting is connected with some artful and unsportsmanlike "dodge." Rabchick, for instance, which are perhaps more plentiful than anything else, are always got at by "calling." The man sets himself down to imitate the bird's own cry, upon a small quill, and as the rabchicks in the neighbourhood come flying up, and settle on a tree within range, are "potted" in succession. Capercailzie are followed into the woods by the sportsmen in a sledge with a fast trotting horse, immediately after the first fall of snow, when they perch on the trees together with the black game; or, in spring, they are stalked in a peculiar manner from tree to tree.

This bird is very wary and shy, and scared at the slightest noise. He perches on the top of a tall pine-tree, and utters a peculiar cry at intervals; while the bird does this he shuts his eyes, and the peasant, who is watching him from a distance, uses the opportunity to get to a nearer shelter, and wait for another cry, when he moves nearer still, until at last he can get within short range of the capercailzie; but he has to be very wary and silent, for the slightest sound, as the crushing of a twig, or a stumbling step, will startle the bird from its perch.

Blackcock are shot in great numbers in the spring, immediately after the disappearance of the snow, when the power of the sun begins to make itself felt. The cocks then come out into the open glades of the woods to fight; and when once they have chosen a spot for this purpose, they return to it morning after morning. Then the peasant, who has marked their rendezvous, goes there in their absence, and raises a sort of hut among the branches of young trees, which he carefully covers with the foliage, making it look as natural as possible. This hut is left there for a few days, until the birds are supposed to have become accustomed to it. Then, when the morning of action is near, a few stuffed hens are cunningly posted among the branches of the trees round about, to convince the real blackcocks of the innocence of the place; and the sportsman hides in his ambush during the night, arranges himself comfortably, makes a few peep-holes to shoot through, and patiently waits for daybreak. With the first approach of dawn, the birds arrive in the twilight, with a great noise, and at once get to business, fighting and challenging each other with a great crowing.

The peasant also gets to business, and, as they come within range, murders them as they stand on the ground, or perch with the stuffed hens on the trees. With the first appearance of the sun above the horizon, the survivors fly off; but while they are on the ground, they take no notice of the shooting. So intent are they upon their fighting among themselves, that I once shot one of a pair that were so engaged, and, when he fell to the gun, his adversary did not even look up, but continued to spur the dead body, until I knocked him over also. In the above way very large bags are made. I have killed as many as seventeen brace in the short interval between daybreak and sunrise.

Wild fowl are shot, as they come to feed in the morning and evening, from hides erected either on a boat moored in the river or lake, or on the shores. They are also bagged in great quantities, sometimes as many as forty or fifty to one gun. Woodcock, snipe, partridges, &c., not being amenable to calls, rarely fall to the peasant's gun. No one who has not been to the country can imagine anything like the abundance of this game, and the splendid day's shooting that can be had upon it. With the help of an old steady dog, a moderately good shot can easily bag between five o'clock and noon, from twenty to thirty brace. I have often known such a man to bring home in August from twenty to twenty-five couple of double snipe in a day; and a greater treat for a gourmand than the flesh of this bird I do not know.

Russia is a wonderful place for meeting enormous flocks of birds of passage. I once passed a lake that had all the water drained out, and noticed nothing on it as I passed; but when I returned a few hours afterwards, the bed of the lake was literally covered with all kinds of large and small birds, which had settled to rest on their migratory flight. It was a curious sight. The birds were so exhausted that they could not get out of our way; but we knocked some down with sticks, and picked them up in our hands.

In the spring time the numerous small islands of the Gulf of Finland, very near to St. Petersburg, are crowded with redwings and ruffs; and it is extraordinary what a number of specimens can be collected there.

I have been told that the study of natural history in Russia has not been much pursued. I am sure it offers a good field to the student of ornithology especially.

Every Russian peasant builds a little wooden bird-cot near his house, which the starlings take possession of upon their arrival in early spring, and occupy until the approaching cold warns them southward to milder climates.

Hares are also very plentiful. They are generally of the blue sort, and very large. The Russians do not care much for them, and therefore seldom shoot them; but sometimes, when snow has been falling in the night and left off before morning, a peasant will follow a hare's tracks through the snow.

At a short distance from the form, the track always describes a very small circuit, and then the peasant makes ready his gun, and soon after stirs up puss with the barrel, and at the same moment blows a hole in her body, which is usually fatal. I have seen a whole cartload of hares taken by boys in the spring time, when the rivers rise and flood the country for many miles. The boys pick out some rising ground above the flood, which gradually diminishes as the water rises, and the hares are, in consequence, driven together in a corner, where the boys follow and knock them down with sticks.

Some of my readers will probably want to know where all this good shooting is to be found, and how they can get it. I can only say that it is to be found almost everywhere, at distances not too great from the towns. Let anybody who wants sport go to Moscow, and at the club there soon get introduced to plenty of landed proprietors, who will put him in the way of getting what he wants. Nobody in Russia thinks of preserving, except the members of a few clubs near St. Petersburg; and not only is the shooting comparatively open to all comers—certainly to any strangers—but hospitality and a hearty welcome are sure to be offered besides.

Within 250 miles of Moscow, I have seen game in greater quantities than anybody can want; and as the journey is performed by rail, this is not too great a distance to travel. I can fancy no more agreeable amusement than that of shooting in such a climate as that of central Russia in the month of August. One is liable to be annoyed by mosquitos, and, for the benefit of sportsmen there and elsewhere, I record my plan of keeping them off. I carried in my waistcoat pocket a small phial of salad oil, in which I had mixed a few drops of oil of tar, and when I found myself among the enemy I rubbed this oil over my hands and face, and scarcely one mosquito would annoy me. The smell of the creosote is not disagreeable, but the insects certainly avoid it.

The large game that I mentioned before are plentiful in the provinces of Vladimir and Nijny Novgorod and Twer.

Hereabouts are plenty of bears, generally two different species, large and small, of the brown bear; black bears are very rarely met with, but I once saw as many as five—two old ones and three cubs—together in one place. The Russian sportsman in chase of a bear sometimes adopts the following plan of getting a shot.

Having found a place where a bear is accustomed to pass, he looks for three trees growing near together, in an arrangement approaching the triangular. He selects trees of such a growth that the top branches of the three joined together will just about support his weight, but are not strong enough individually for the bear to climb up after him.

Among these three tree tops he makes himself a comfortable hiding-place, and then fastens a cow-bell to a tree in the neighbourhood, holding a string from the cow-bell in his hand.

When this is arranged, he climbs to his hiding-place as well as he can with his gun, and begins to ring the cow-bell by pulling the string. The bear, when he hears the cow-bell, begins to think of beef, and comes stealthily towards the sound in search of a meal. It is curious to watch him when he comes under the bell and cannot find the cow; his head twists round and round like a windmill in motion; but presently some movement in the hiding-place attracts his attention, and he will come right underneath it and look straight up. Now is the time to give him the contents of your gun ; and if the peasant's gun will go off (which it does about once in ten trials), it is a bad chance for Bruin, as the gun will probably contain, on the top of a double charge of powder, something like two bullets, a lump of iron, a small pebble or two, and perhaps the ramrod. If the bear should be only wounded by the discharge, he will wait about the place a long time for his revenge; in which case the Mujik must stay in the tree, either till the bear goes away of his own accord, or the Mujik's friends arrive and frighten him off.

As to all the traveller's tales about the ferocity of the bear and his proneness to attack men, I can only say that I have always found the greatest difficulty in getting near a bear. As a rule he is off at the first notice he gets of your neighbourhood.

So it is with wolves also. I have seen a great many in all situations on all sorts of occasions, and I never saw but one that showed any disposition to attack either myself or the horses in my Tarentasse.

The peasants sometimes capture a bear in his winter quarters, detecting these by discoloration or air-holes in the snow at the opening of their caves. A number of peasants, armed with guns, poles, &c., surround the spot, and rouse the sleeping animal by calling him, or, if necessary, by stirring him up with a pole. When at last, sleepy and stupid, the bear puts his head out of the hole, all the company fire at him and run away, returning after a time to see the result, and to repeat the attack if their first attempt has been unsuccessful. But bears taken during the hibernation are not worth having. They are exceedingly lean, and their hides are ragged and thin.

It is curious to notice the aversion that the bear has to music. I had a couple of young bears about my house, which were constantly in our sitting-rooms, but, immediately that anybody began to play the piano, they began to howl and cry, and nothing could quiet them until they were beyond hearing of the music.

I have only heard of two instances of bears doing harm to anybody. In one case, some men who were cutting wood in a forest were told by a boy that he had seen a bear. It was winter time, and the bear, asleep in his hole, had probably been awakened by the noise made by the wood-cutters.

One of the men went to the hole, and the bear put his head out, whereupon the man tapped the bear on the head with the axe, and the bear retaliated at once by scalping the man. Next day, near the same place, some peasants saw a bear (it must have been the same one) sitting half asleep in the middle of the road. As he did not move out of the way, the driver went up to the bear and flogged him with his whip, whereupon this Red Indian of a Bruin scalped him also.

Both these men (although their scalps were completely gone) were, I am glad to say, cured in our hospital.

Lynxes, or, as the Russians call them, wild cats, are often seen when the great battues are made. On such an occasion I was fortunate to see one. It was at a battue about forty miles from St. Petersburg. I was standing waiting in my place, tired and rather dozing than otherwise, and I daresay missing a number of chances of a shot, when I suddenly woke up to a state of liveliness on hearing the breaking of twigs near at hand. Presently I saw something coming towards me that startled me, and

I began to think I must still be asleep and dreaming, for before me was an animal such as I had never before seen in a wild state. I imagined it to be a young tiger or leopard; it was the size of a small mastiff, very strong in the feet and legs, having a broad chest, a large head, and of a reddish-grey colour, spotted.

I had never expected to see such an animal, and was so much astonished that it did not occur to me to fire; which was fortunate, in fact, as my gun was only charged with No. 4 shot, and firing this into such an animal would have been useless. He trotted slowly off, and as I looked after him, I apprehended at last that I had had the fortune to see a lynx at close quarters, but I never saw another. A good many bears and elks are trapped by the peasants in large gins. The Russian peasant, who likes this sport amazingly, is a wonderful hand at a trap, which he will rarely set without catching something. He will follow the tracks of a herd of elk for week after week, until he discovers where they have chosen for themselves a resting-place. Near this place, upon some path which the elks have made, and will use daily, the hunter sets his gin and makes it fast to a tree with a thick strong chain, then covers all lightly with leaves and earth.

Among the troop of animals crowding along the path, one is sure to tread on the fatal snare and fall a victim to the hunter, if he does not meet a still worse fate, poor beast, and escape leaving his foot in the snare, which happens very often. I do not know whether elks survive this cruel mutilation, but I know that bears do, as I once shot one which had lost its foot in that way, and the animal was perfectly cured, running about on three feet almost as well as if he had four.

When a bear is caught by the foot, he will even try to bite it off above the trap. Of this I have also seen an instance in my own experience; having shot a bear in a trap, whose leg we found nearly bitten through above where it had been caught.

Very capital sport is wolf shooting in Russia. The sportsmen set off in a large sledge, preceded by a smaller sledge, in which are two men, one of whom holds the reins while another carries a live pig in his arms; at the bottom of the sledge is another pig muffled in a bag. Behind your own sledge you trail a rope, about thirty yards long, with a wisp of hay at the end of it, which dances about like something alive over the inequalities of the snow. Away the two sledges gallop, not in the woods, but on the plains in the neighbourhood of villages; the man in the leading sledge pinches his pig's ear, and the pig wakes the echoes with his shrieks, which resound far and wide through the silent frosty night. Moonlight nights are necessarily chosen for this amusement, when the wolves can be seen from a great distance. At first they appear like a crowd of bounding shadows; and as their gaunt active forms become more and more outlined against the snow, the excitement becomes intense. The sledges, however, continue their course to the music of the screams of the pig, for if they were stopped the herd of wolves would be dispersed in a minute. At last the troop perceive the bounding wisp of hay, and come down towards it with a rush, while the air resounds with their short, yelping bark, sounding chorus to the squealing pigs.

This is the critical moment; sometimes they detect the imposture of the hay, and turn tail at a safe distance: more often they cannot resist the hope of pork, and on they come within range. Then, at a given moment, all the guns in the sledge are emptied on them, and all but the dead or wounded disperse like magic. Apart from the novel sensation of being hunted by your game, the act of shooting straight is by no means easy under the circumstances.

The roads in the snow are never quite even, and the sledge is sure to be rocking from side to side. It is thus somewhat difficult to hold a gun straight; and you must of necessity shoot running, because the instant that the sledge is stopped, the wolves are gone out of range like lightning.

As to jumping out of the sledge in motion, that is sometimes done; but it is not an easy thing to do, encumbered as you must be with a heavy fur coat and colossal boots loose and lined with fur.

I have heard it said that wolves are very cunning; now I do not think so, and for the following reason : I once fastened on my trailing rope two wisps of hay instead of one only, at a distance of about ten yards apart, wishing to see what a wolf would do when he came to the first for pork and found it "gammon."

To my surprise, a wolf bounded up to the first piece of hay, smelt it, and immediately, instead of turning tail, pounced towards the second wisp, before he reached which, however, he was rewarded for his stupidity by the contents of my gun.

On the other hand, I have always found that we were sure to draw a blank, let our pig squeak ever so melodiously, if we went to any neighbourhood where we had shot, say, a week previously, and had let any wounded wolves escape us.

The best bait of all for catching wolves is

a live dog. This animal to a wolf is an irresistible temptation. If one can only train a dog to run about twenty yards behind a sledge, and bark as he runs; and, when the wolves come upon him, to draw gradually nearer and nearer to the sledge, all the wolves in the neighbourhood may be exterminated.

I believe that wolves travel great distances in search of food. I once particularly noticed in a pack a large wolf, who had only half a tail, which he carried in a very peculiar manner; and on the following night I saw him again at a distance of more than thirty miles from the spot where I had seen him on the previous one.

They also hunt wolves by battues, employing sometimes as many as two hundred beaters. But it is cold and tame sport to wait on one spot until something comes towards you.

Wolves appear to be difficult to tame. I have tried to do so with several young ones, but I never succeeded. They invariably strangle themselves in their collars and chains; but they are tamed sometimes. At Ekaterienberg I saw two chained up in a yard in the house of the head of the Mining Department, which do the duty of watch-dogs; and are tame enough to allow those who know them to go up to and pat them.

In the Oural are what are called by the natives wild goats; they are pretty plentiful, I believe, but I was never fortunate enough to see one of them. I cannot think, however, they are goats. They are most probably a species of deer. The roe-deer, in fact, is very plentiful in the southern parts of the Oural Mountains, in the neighbourhood of Ufallen.

The fishing in Russia is *nil*. There are

plenty of fish, which are not worth angling for, excepting the pike; and as the largest of these are in the lakes, which are always more or less full of stumps and roots of trees, it is impossible to spin for them; or the constant loss and breakage of your tackle takes away all the pleasure of the sport. In the Oural there are a few trout in some of the streams, which we should call black, or mountain trout, but not in sufficient quantity to make fishing for them worth while.

Far away in the Oural there are grayling worth fishing for, but this is too remote to mention.

In most of the northern rivers, and in the Volga, we find the sterlet, a fish remarkable for the richness of its flavour, which certainly cannot be overrated; but they offer no sport to the angler.

With the above exceptions, the fish are all

common white fish, such as roach, rudd, bleak, &c.; these abound in rivers and lakes; and as the Russians are great fish eaters in consequence of their frequent fasts, large quantities are taken. It is all the same to a Russian how and when he takes them, they are never out of season: and, as I have often seen nets made of bass-mats, it is wonderful that any fish are left, as fry and all go into the pot.

In the Neva a good many salmon are taken by netting, but it is not a river that can be fished with the rod.

Also in the river Oural, and some of the Siberian rivers, there are vast quantities of salmon; but these places are at present too far off, and inaccessible to tempt the sportsman.

Finland has also plenty of trout.

The Russians are clever at fishing with the net. They may be seen on a frozen lake in the winter in a regular surveying party, measuring here, digging holes there, and planting red flags in another place; the result of which scientific proceedings is, that they will empty the lake of every fin of fish that it contains.

The greatest part of the fish, which may be called the staple article of food in the fast times, comes from the lower ends of the Volga and the Don; I mean such fish as sturgeon, beluga, accitrina, &c., which are all large fish, weighing from 60 lb. upwards.

All over Russia a good many fish are taken, as in all northern countries by spearing; and a very pleasant amusement it is on a still summer night, to sit and watch the fires on the water; and while you admire their glowing reflection and listen to the plaintive songs of the distant fishermen (for all Russian music has a very peculiar plaintive sound), you can almost envy the quiet and contented life of the Russian Mujik.

The people have very numerous holidays. According to the calendar these ought to come about twice a day, but they are practically reduced to at least forty in the year, not including Sundays. But they have very few amusements. Sometimes, but very seldom, a few boys may be seen playing a game something like hockey. Generally, on a holiday, the girls get together in groups and amuse themselves by singing their mournful national songs. But the grown up people lounge about with idle hands, doing literally nothing; sit on the ledge outside the house; or lie flat on their faces to have their heads cleaned by the rest. (Another strikingly oriental practice). Some of the men will be taking their fit of drunkenness at the Traktir on every holiday. Like all people who are fond of shirking their work on any pretence, they do not know what to do with themselves without it. If they were men who had energy to find rational amusement, they would not require so many holidays, and would be ashamed to make their religious observances a mere pretext for idleness and debauchery. As it is, they doze away their holidays in complete inactivity; even in winter, when one would think that they must do something to keep themselves warm, it is all the same. They lounge about listlessly with nothing to do and nothing to say.

Occasionally an individual is seen on the ice hills; but, as a general rule, if you go to the expense of making one of those very Russian institutions, you will very seldom see it used.

In other oriental countries, where the

people cannot read, they are fond of having stories told them; but this is not a general amusement with the Mujiks. I have noticed a group, now and then listening to some narrative, but the practice is by no means common.

In every rank of society the boys and girls are without any sort of games by which they can amuse themselves rationally. Excepting a mild game at ball, they know nothing of the sort, and a fight between boys is an unheard-of thing; the boys are throughout too effeminately reared, as I have remarked in another place.

The carnival is a great time for the Russians. Then, in the larger Zavods (industrial villages), all the population promenade in all sorts of vehicles, from the master in his well-appointed sledge, to the labouring miner in his clumsy ore cart. In the evening they all disguise themselves in masks and fancy dresses; and making the round of the village houses, dance a little, drink a little, and pick up an accession to their party at every house.

It is now three years since I entertained such an assembly in my house in a great Zavod village.

The servants decorated the great hall for the occasion; the village band — a violin and violoncello — were in attendance, tuned and impatient to begin before the first maskers arrived. These represented a man leading a dancing bear. The bear leader was got up in the proper costume, with regular professional tom-tom; and the bear wore his skin like an old hand. These two maskers were two of my " Dvorniks " (house porters).

They were followed by all the others in a crowd. First, a ferocious little gentleman, in a uniform rather postal than military, carrying a sword which he tells me decapitated ever so many Turks in the Crimean war, and with a helmet said to be the spoil of an English dragoon, but plainly that of the fireman who stands bareheaded by the door. It is delightful to see this courteous warrior drink a glass of champagne, with the masked and dominoed lady in the white kid gloves who leans on his arm. It is amazing to be told that the warrior is my butler's son,—a warehouseman in the works at 12s. 6d. a week,— and his fair companion one of the work girls of the house. Presently the band of stringed instruments strike up a dance, and the Mujiks fall into position for a French quadrille. This they perform decorously and seriously, without noise or vulgarity; in fact, as a quadrille should be danced—solemnly.

The quadrille finished, a lady is prevailed

upon to sing, and she gives us, to piano accompaniment, a plaintive Russian melody, sung with precision and feeling in a very musical voice. My house, by this time, is crowded with the company of the villagers continually arriving and leaving. A sideboard has been laid out with light eatables and drinkables, including champagne, and here there is no more crowding or noise than elsewhere. The whole proceeding from beginning to end, was perfect in exemplary decency and good behaviour; and yet there were as many as 250 masked people in the house, and every one of them had been a " serf." An Englishman who was visiting me at the time, exclaimed:—" Why, this is the most wonderful sight I have ever beheld ! "

A similar taste of the people is for illuminations, which they are very fond of. It is a pretty sight on Easter-day, to see the churches completely covered with little lamps, that trace out the lines of their architecture against the sky.

The priests have no hand in this decoration, which is entirely managed by the people. The mayor generally goes round, and begs on behalf of the community for the necessary quantity of tallow for the purpose.

The bazaars — as their weekly markets are called — are very interesting; generally held upon a Sunday in the village of the greatest importance within a radius of fifty versts. In our village — which was the greatest centre of industry for very many miles—one of the largest bazaars was held: always on a Sunday, when about 5,000 strangers would assemble.

There would always be more in winter than in summer, because of the better roads. It is not only the people who have business to do who come to these gatherings, but all who can do so come also,—for the sake of company, to have a chat with their friends, and to see "the world." The peasants in their best suits of clothes, and the women in their liveliest colours, come in troops along all the high roads, radiating towards the fair. At a short distance from the bazaar, the women sit down to put on their clean shoes and stockings, which they have carried hitherto, and take off again at the same spot when they turn their steps homeward in the evening. There is no limit to the variety of articles bought and sold at these bazaars; not only all articles of food, but of dress also: in fact, everything that is useful, not to the peasantry alone, but to the middle classes, including articles of ornament and amusement for the interior of decent households. Some of the very national manufactures are well worth notice. The pottery articles, the water bottles, mugs and jugs, are often quite classically modelled from patterns handed down from sire to son through many generations. These potteries are quaintly coloured in oriental fashion. In wood they make beautiful bowls for cooking and eating, such as the Mujik always uses at home; but these are all curiously painted and varnished, which seems less clean and nice than the plain wood; and wooden trays, which are like Japan ware, and in colour almost rival the commoner sorts. Other antique looking objects of painted wood, are the tops made to fix on to their spinning machines. Sometimes in these bazaars, among old curiosities, may be picked up quaint and ancient picture images of the saints, which, however, are never for sale. That would be irreligious, but the owner of them would not object to *exchange* them for other commodities, or money.

A good deal of vodky is consumed at these gatherings of the peasants; but they are cheerful and good-tempered in their cups—an example in this respect to our English peasants: one never sees any quarrelling or brawling, and all who are not occupied in dealing, are busy in discussing the affairs of their several villages.

A great deal of grain, seed, and other produce is brought to the bazaars, where the small merchants collect a great quantity of the produce that is ultimately exported. The peasants are very honest in their dealings; they will sell cartloads of stuff by one sample, and always deliver what they sell of equal quality. In this I think they are an example to the peasants of many other countries. The bazaars, or the places where they are held, are generally the property of the owners of the village, to whom every cart that enters pays a small tax, and the vendors of general goods pay a rent for the ground they occupy with their stores.

The ground is often so farmed out and sub-let by some village speculator.

The owner of the soil has another similar privilege with respect to licensing vodky dealers, who cannot obtain their patent from the Crown without the license first had of the proprietor.

Large sums are paid for these licenses in places where much money circulates.

From our head village, with a fixed population of not more than 4,000 souls, we received £250 a year for letting licenses to sell vodky.

It is astonishing to see what can be bought in these villages. I know one with a population of 4,000 (a thousand miles from St. Petersburg), in the shops of which can be bought almost everything that you can wish for, including such things as black velvet, English cloth, French silks, truffles, champagne, Lafitte, and good cigars!

CHAPTER VII.

MANUFACTURES AND TRADE.

PROBABLY the manufacture which fifty years ago was the most important one in Russia, referred to metals. Let me dwell for a moment on its history.

About 180 years ago there lived two blacksmiths at Tula, who had heard of the immense quantities of iron that lay, scarcely covered by the soil, throughout the Empire; of the abundant forests, that seemed to offer an inexhaustible supply of fuel; and of the advantages offered by the Government to any who would take in hand the development of those stores of wealth.

The names of the two blacksmiths, Demidoff and Botacheff, are now household words through the length and breadth of the Empire. Both were men of great genius and extraordinary energy; when one looks at the work they did, and consider the difficulties they had to contend with, we do not know whether most to admire, the magnitude and boldness of their conceptions or the patient energy and perseverance of their conduct. They both prospered nearly alike.

Demidoff, branching out from his first works which he established at Neviansk, in the north of the Oural, had soon availed himself of every spot where water could be collected, and founded an iron works there.

No authentic record, I believe, exists, of the precise number of foundries which he built; but Botacheff, who, it is known, followed closely in his wake, left behind him twenty-five large works, extending over something like a million and a half of acres, and employing a population of upwards of fifty thousand souls.

After the death of Demidoff and Botacheff, their properties were cut up and divided, constantly increased by their successors, and again partitioned in another generation; and so the iron industry of Russia has spread from those two fountain-heads to its present great proportions. Copper mining was not undertaken in the country until a later date. The now famous mine of Nijny Tagil, the first of any importance that was opened, was not worked on until 1814. It was on the site of one of Demidoff's original works, and is owned by the descendants of Demidoff's family to this day. It was soon discovered that all the country, on the Asiatic side of the Oural mountains, from a point a long way to the north of Tagil to another close upon

Orenburg in the south, abounded with copper ore. A number of mines were quickly opened on this line of country and many copper works erected.

So much for the rise and progress of the mineral industry. We have now to consider its decline and fall, for it has fallen off to a great extent from its greatest development. The immediate descendants of the two great blacksmiths, of Demidoff and of Botacheff, found themselves enormously wealthy, beyond all necessity of enterprise or exertion. They acquired great influence in the Empire, were raised to the nobility, and appointed to high offices of state by the Imperial Government. Their attention was thus withdrawn from the sources of their greatness, and the management of their mines left to the hands of subordinates, deteriorated. As time rolled on, other people began to open copper mines and iron foundries, in competition with theirs; prices and profits were reduced, but the two families, accustomed to greatness, neither applied themselves to maintain the efficiency of their mines, nor to reduce their personal expenditure which exceeded the incomes they derived from them. They soon began to borrow large sums on the mortgage of their properties, chiefly to the Government, but in part to anybody who would make them a loan.

The families of the Demidoffs and Botacheffs, in their system of borrowing at all hands, were soon embarrassed to meet the payments of interest as they fell due; and Government readily took advantage of their default, by taking the estates and works of the insolvent families into its own management; nominally, still for the benefit of the proprietors, but in the first place for the satisfaction of the claims of the Government, under the control of a Committee of Tutelage, or so-called, "*Tutor.*" From this time the ruin of the old mining families was very rapid, and is now, in many cases, complete, so that the nominal owners of vast properties are in fact quite impoverished. The system of government tutelage never answered in the management of mines, and from the time it became common, the profits derived from the mines have diminished and the works deteriorated.

Year after year the department of mines, although possessing some of the richest and most convenient works, which ought, under proper management to have yielded a great revenue, found an increasing balance at the debit of their accounts.

Of course the corruption inseparable from Russian official life was the cause of the failure of the tutelage system. Large profits were, in fact, earned by the mines, but these never reached the coffers of the Government. As usual, the department underpaid its officers, whose principal energies were consequently directed to the earning of their own living, by "commissions," on the affairs entrusted to them, or otherwise. It is difficult to condemn them, knowing that their salaries were not enough for them to live upon. The system was radically wrong. I have known personally many of the higher officers among these men, who would conscientiously exhaust their energies in the attempt to check the peculations of their subordinates; but they were too few for their duties, spread over so vast an expanse of country.

The whole system of government traffic and manufacture is rotten throughout. Even where a manager is capable and anxious to do his duty, he is baffled by the process of red-tapeism, which all his requirements have to undergo, and induced to give up energising in disgust. I knew an officer, who, in other matters a perfectly honourable man, said to me in reference to his works, as he was showing them to me,—

"You must not expect to see here such good work as you are accustomed to. The fact is, the Government offers us no inducement to work. Here am I, after long services, after rising step by step to my present rank, in the receipt of seventy roubles (about £10) a month, and the responsibility of the whole of this concern upon me. You see, I just make it pay—and, in fact, that is all I care about. If I were to double the profits, I should not be thanked."

Whatever may be thought of the morality of this sentiment, it is an extremely natural one. It is a rule or custom of the service, that the manager of a government works keeps his position so long only as he can "make both ends meet;" but if once he required help, however meritorious he may be, or however prudent his management, he is promptly superseded. Consequently the most ingenious manœuvres are resorted to by managers of unremunerative concerns, to make them appear in the books to be self-supporting. In the course of my inquiries at one of the government works, originally built by the great Demidoff, now practically ruined, I came to the conclusion that the cost of the iron that was made there was considerably in excess of the price it could be sold at. I pointed this out to the manager, and asked for an explanation. He admitted at once the fact that the property was ruined beyond redemption; but, he said,—

"I can still return a profit to the Government."

When I pressed him on the subject, he added,—

"Yes, I don't make the profit out of my manufacture; but my brother is the manager of some government works not far from here, and he buys my raw iron."

The fact was, his brother paid him a sufficient price for his raw iron — about double its marketable value—to enable him to cover the losses on his manufacture, and still return a nominal profit to the Government, and thus retain his appointment—and so the Government was swindled annually out of a large sum of money for the good of his family. These abuses are worthy of serious attention, by reason of the great political importance of the mining question to the Russian empire. Many thousands of the population, spread over immense extent of country, have nothing but the mines to depend upon for their livelihood. From father to son, now through several generations, these people have lived by mining, and know nothing else, and are fit for no other industry. So long as there is work to be had at the mines and foundries, the people are contented and comfortable; but when these come to a standstill, the result is starvation, discontent, and finally uproar.

In some parts of Siberia difficulties have arisen, quite recently, from such a cause; and the peasantry have refused to pay the taxes. In one large Zavod village, with a population of 12,000 souls, these disturbances have become serious. Several hundreds of the people stoutly refused to pay the amount of taxes they were rated at; and this was the reason they gave, they said,—

"A man had been round to them all with a book, written in letters of gold, which told them they were not to pay these taxes."

Now, these people lived upon some of the

works, which are in process of being ruined by a Government tutelage. If the works had been going forward as they should do, the people would have had no time to care for such nonsense as the above.

The Government are now awake to the necessity of introducing complete reform in the Department of Mines, and have determined to get rid not only of all the private works, which have come to them by mortgage, but also of those set in operation by themselves; and only to reserve one or two which are serviceable, in a manner, as arsenals.

The "works," as they are always called in Russia, are of a character peculiar to the country, and such as are not to be met with in other parts of the world; in their enormous proportions, and their *modus operandi*, they are a peculiarly Russian institution.

Many of the establishments extend their operations over a space containing from three-quarters of a million to a million and a half English acres; erect their works here and there, where a favourable site exists, and thus form little principalities, containing numerous villages, which are entirely supported by the labour of the mines. It is easy to perceive that the proprietor of such an estate has immense influence over his dependent people, and that great misery is caused when the "works" are badly, and great comfort and happiness to the people when they are well, managed.

In the olden times the "Barrin" lived in almost princely style — in a palace surrounded by highly ornamental gardens and extensive parks, laid out with the most excellent taste. In his gardens were hot-houses, vineries, and orange-houses, erected at great expense. Frequently he had a private theatre of his own, a band of music in constant attendance; and I know of at least one of the ironmasters of the last generation, who supported a company of actors and actresses, collected from among his own Mujiks, whom he sent to Moscow and St. Petersburg to be educated expressly for his own stage. Such a man, in the days of serfdom, had all the state and authority of a monarch, enjoying unlimited and irresponsible power among his servile dependents. Of course, the condition of these last was regulated by the character or caprice of their master: some were cruel; but, on the other hand, some governed their people with a kindness and discretion wonderful to think of in men brought up as they had been. As an instance of cruelty, I know of a proprietor who caused a man, who had offended him, to be locked up in an iron cage, and kept him confined in it for a length of time.

At last, while he was absent on a journey, the case of his wretched prisoner came to the knowledge of the governor of his province. The governor caused the man, cage and all, to be brought to the government town. He also despatched a messenger to intercept the tyrannical proprietor on the road, with an invitation to dinner. This the proprietor, flattered by the courtesy, accepted very willingly, and presented himself at the government house at the appointed time.

There was a curious fashion in Russia at that time of keeping live quails, whose notes were greatly admired by connoisseurs in the peculiar fancy. The governor was famous for his collection of these singing birds—the dinner was very good, and the company very merry.

After the cloth was removed, the governor addressed his guest,—

"Now, Ivan Simonovitch, I know you are very fond of quails; and I have a beauty, which I don't mind selling you."

"Very well, excellency; if the bird is not too dear, I will buy him of you."

"Bring in the quail," said his excellency to the attendants.

A very ordinary sort of bird, in a wooden cage, was introduced.

"Now I wan't to sell you that bird for ten thousand roubles," said the governor.

The ironmaster could not understand the joke, but declined the bargain, as he thought the bird was a little too dear.

"Well," said the governor, "I will show you a better bird than that, and I think you'll buy him."

"Have the other quail brought in."

Folding-doors flew open, and the iron cage with its miserable captive was set down before the astonished guest.

"Now," said the governor, "what do you think of that for a quail? but this is a very expensive bird; I want 20,000 roubles for him!"

"All right," said the alarmed proprietor; "I will buy this one, send him down to my works without the cage, and your messenger shall bring back the amount."

The matter was thus pleasantly settled, and the company adjourned in undisturbed harmony to their papirosses and coffee.

History does not add that the poor peasant benefited by any part of the 20,000 roubles.

The gold workings are important enough to have a great influence on the future wealth of the nation.

Until quite recently the Crown, as owner of the soil, kept the monopoly of digging for gold over a great extent of country, and the work was in consequence badly done; a great deal of the gold was stolen; and, what was worse, the rest was negligently washed and much wasted.

In this matter of gold digging as in every branch of industry we consider, our reflections always lead us naturally to the conclusion, that free-trade and the complete abolition of the absurd restrictions remaining on industrial enterprise, will effect an incalculable change in the wealth and resources of the country, which nobody even among the most intelligent Russians themselves is able to measure as yet.

I have mentioned Russia's wealth in one of the subjects of our own country's boasting—iron; and could show that she possesses also another of our resources of wealth in the various kinds of coal scattered about her vast territory. From the black coal on the Kama, near Perm, the immense deposits of the Don basin, the anthracite of the Sea of

Azov, to the common gas coal found in the Caucasian mountains and on the borders of the Caspian Sea. With similar stores of such wealth, Britain has once climbed to the supreme rank in commerce, and those who are watching the social progress of Russia predict a like career of prosperity for her.

The manufacturing industry of Russia increases rapidly, whilst it is curious to observe, that although a Russian workman is capable of imitating everything that is shown to him, his power of initiation is generally nil. Still, there are manufactures in which the Russians excel.

Their printed cloths, for instance, are unique, well made, and of good design; well known in the eastern markets throughout Central Asia and China.

In the manufacture of woollen goods also they have made some progress, and a very respectable kind of cloth is now produced in

Russia, which has superseded the manufacture of our own country in many Oriental markets. China, Afghanistan, Persia, and the north-western borders of India are now supplied with the produce of Russian looms, which, if not so good in quality, is as well liked by the Eastern peoples as English cloth, and is considerably cheaper, taking quality for quality.

Her manufactures in the precious metals are celebrated throughout the world for elegance and beauty. Her productions in leather are unrivalled, and the versatility of her manufacturing genius is so unbounded, that it would be difficult to name an article of modern invention that is not made somewhere or other in the Empire.

And with all this, it must still be remembered that the manufacturing industry of Russia is not yet fifty years old. It required nursing at first under a system of protection, but is now so far developed as to admit a great deal of free competition, and the gradual introduction of a liberal policy.

The great annual fairs of Nijny Novgorod and Irbit are now crowded with Russian manufactures. In the former alone the turnover exceeds seventeen millions of pounds.

Everything is now done to stimulate trade; every inducement held out to encourage manufacture; a more liberal tariff obliges the manufacturers to compete closely with the foreigner; and Russia is straining every nerve to be as much as possible independent of the world for useful manufactures.

The anomalies that used to be seen are passing away; for instance, raw skins would be sent from the same place as the bark grew to tan them with; both were sold at the fair at Nijny? (mind, only once a year), taken somewhere to be tanned, and then ready leather sent back perhaps a thousand miles, to the place where they came from, to be sold as finished skins.

Tallow would be sent two thousand versts from where it was produced to be made into candles, and these returned to where the tallow came from; now the people are arousing themselves, and many manufactories are springing up.

The Russians can adapt themselves to any work. The English manager of a British-owned paper-mill, which even *I* was astonished to find established amongst the Oural mountains, was recounting to me that in England it was thought necessary for a man to have served his time for a term of years to make him a good workman; but that three months made his men capital paper-makers, just as good as Englishmen of the same class.

Although the principal manufactories in

the interior are in the hands of Russians, Russians, as a rule, do not like commencing any new industry, and are shy of doing so; this is why it is so desirable for the Government to encourage foreigners to settle in the country, as I have before remarked, and these once having set the example, it will be followed; but one must not look to Russians to commence.

At one time almost all the managers, and what may be called leading hands in Russian manufactories, were foreigners, either English or German; but as these gradually got into business for themselves, their places were filled by natives. This is as it should be, for without doubt a Russian workman generally prefers a native to a foreign master.

Russian manufactured articles are cheap, and in several, quality for quality, she can successfully compete with foreign nations; but, generally, her goods are not made for those markets which require the best articles. Russia looks to the East to be her greatest customer, and it is for the Eastern market that articles are specially made by her.

As a matter of course, as her trade increases, her exports will materially increase, and with them her importations of raw material.

A better system is adopted of doing business, the terms of credit are lessened, and increased confidence amongst traders is visible.

Greatly in praise of Russian probity is it, that the long credits given were not much abused: a merchant, for instance, who bought goods of an internal trader, was in the habit in many cases of paying all the money in advance to the seller, who would go thousands of miles away to collect his wares; this man would never be seen again until a year afterwards, when he returned with the goods, and it rarely happened that he failed to complete his bargain. In selling imported goods to the country dealers, a credit of fifteen or eighteen months was very generally given. A great portion of the business even now done at Nijny and Irbit fairs is on the terms of giving the goods, and taking payment for them at the next fair.

In the absence of railways it was impossible to do business otherwise; the goods were so long in getting to their destination, that under a year a buyer could not get a return.

Fabrics are now springing up fitted with native made machinery. Branches of industry are started, which before were thought to be impossible for Russian ingenuity to master, and trade flourishes as it never flourished before. Ever since the Crimean war, the amount of the interchange of commodities has been increasing; this, in the face of a tariff that was the worst in Europe, must show what a power this Empire has in herself.

I have always held the idea that the increase of railways in the south of Russia would considerably influence the price of wheat in Western Europe, and that in consequence Russia would turn out a powerful rival to America in the quantity the two countries supplied to England. The effect of the railways has hardly began to be felt, and yet the imports of wheat from Russia to this country during the past year have exceeded by one-third those of the preceding one.

For one article of manufacture, that of sugar from beetroot, Russia possesses more establishments than any other country in the world, true I shall be told that this industry has become necessary, in consequence of the import duty on foreign sugars being prohibitory. I admit it, but still it shows that as the Russians can go ahead in this production, they can do so in other things.

As a proof, the imports of sugar to Russia have fallen off from 7,000,000 roubles in 1866 to 800,000 roubles last year.

Look what they have done in cotton spinning; there are now upwards of three hundred establishments in which this staple is prepared, and where something like four hundred thousand bales of cotton are worked up annually. The import of raw cotton last year was one quarter more than in 1868.

The productions in this article are very creditable, the prints capital in quality and beautiful in design. I think, taking the same quality, the designs are far prettier and neater than our own, and from experience the Russian prints wear as well as ours.

The manufacture of silk has attained considerable proportions, and in Moscow and the neighbourhood, are some two hundred establishments where this industry is developing itself; here the quality, as a rule, is not so good as the foreign make, and there is much room for improvement; satins are however made in Moscow superior to French manufactured ones.

All commerce is on the advance, and no one in travelling can fail to be struck with the advantages which offer for the export in increasing quantities, of various articles when the facilities of transport come into more general operation: such, for instance, as linseed, hemp, flax, rape-seed, tallow, leather, &c.

Banks are now being established in many towns. The Bank of State is also increasing the number of its branches, this all gives a great impetus to commerce and causes money to circulate more freely; this is one of the things much wanted. Banking institutions used to be so few and far between, that small money was very difficult to obtain; I do not mean specie, but notes; this of itself was a great drawback amongst small traders.

The improvements in a country like Russia must be more observed by the traveller than by reference to statistics, which are necessarily very imperfect; the extent of country is so great and the ignorance of the officials in many parts equally so, that the most curious absurdities are to be seen very often in the returns.

I have always considered one great sign of the improvements in the general manufactures of a country, is to be noticed in watching how they improve in the manufacture of small articles. Now it may appear trivial to many observers, but I mention such little things as small cutlery, pins, tapes, cottons, even lucifer matches, hooks and eyes, elastics, and other such bagatelles, that have in the last few years much improved.

CHAPTER VIII.

WAYS AND COMMUNICATIONS.

BEFORE the introduction of railways, the system of water communication throughout Russia was already very wonderfully effective and complete. Most of the navigable rivers were connected by a system of canals so perfect that she commanded a safe and inexpensive means of direct carriage, by which her grain could be sent from the south to the north of Europe, and her mineral productions from Siberia to the port of Cronstadt; and the same barges that loaded metals in the Oural mountains could discharge their cargoes at choice either at Cronstadt or Astrakhan. Excepting the distance across the Oural range, between Tiumen in Siberia and the river Kama in European Russia, and other smaller breaks, the water communication from east to west was facile across the Empire; that is to say, from the Neva to the Amoor, from the Black Sea to that of Japan! Tea and other China produce came great part of their journey into Russia by water carriage; and from other nations, lying on the eastern and south-eastern frontiers, she already received a considerable carrying trade.

Now, although this method of transport was cheap and convenient, and did very well in our grandfathers' slower days, yet the loss of time in the delivery of the more valuable kinds of merchandise was a considerable drawback to trade, and as time went on there arose a great cry for railways. This cry has been wonderfully responded to during the past few years—to such an extent as can hardly be believed.

The first railway—that from St. Petersburg to Tsarskoe Selo—was commenced in 1836, and is quite a short line. It was followed in 1837 by the Petersburg-Moscow road; and this again by the Warsaw-Vienna in 1859. So that in twenty years there were only about 950 versts of railroad made. But from the year 1861 the Russians have made up for the time lost before. Commencing then from 1861 to the present time, there have been actually finished about 10,000 versts, and there are now in course of construction some 4,000 versts besides; amounting together to about 9,000 miles!

Doubtless, one thing that facilitated the making of these railroads was the speculative mania raging on the St. Petersburg exchange two years ago, and hence the desire of everyone to obtain shares in the different companies. As a result of this speculation, the two most remarkable examples were those of the Kineshma-Ivanovo Railway, which invited subscriptions for 12,000 shares, and received application for three and a half million, and the company for transport of goods, called "Dvigatel," which applied to the public for 500,000 roubles, and received applications for sixty-four millions, all paid up at the time of application.

Railways are now in active operation from St. Petersburg to Odessa, to the Azov, and to the Volga among the great corn-producing countries of central Russia. Direct routes are laid from Moscow to Western Europe. Poland is opened up, and the great corn marts of Moorshansk and Rybinsk are connected with ports of shipment, which fact alone has given an impetus to the corn trade, that must affect the price of bread in Western

Europe. With one more railway across the hiatus I have already alluded to—from Tobol in Siberia to the Kama in Europe—the continuity of connection between the West of Europe and the extreme eastern limits of Asia will be through the whole breadth of Russia complete and direct! From Samara again, the line now being laid across the steppe towards Orenburg, will facilitate the communication with Central Asia.

A railway across the Caucasus will connect the Black Sea with the Caspian, and bring Persia into closer connection with the South of Europe; and another line from the Caspian to the Sea of Aral, will make it a short journey from St. Petersburg to Khiva. When Russia controls all these proposed lines of communication, her influence in the commerce and policy of Asia must needs be immensely increased.

But the navigation of her rivers continues

to increase; every year the number is added to of the steamers that ply on them. Strangers would be surprised at the elegance and comfort of the passenger steamers of the Volga, that ply to Czaritzin, or even to Astrakhan.

Steam-tugs, also, have superseded the extraordinary, clumsy, and slow mode of progression formerly in use upon the rivers. Imagine a large barge, with a house on deck, in which the captain and his family live, and a sort of shed abaft for the men, to shelter in also. On the fore part of the deck is an enormous capstan, worked sometimes by men, sometimes by horses. A large anchor is put into a tender, which then rows with it some distance ahead of the barge, and throws it overboard. It is attached to the barge by a very thick cable, which is hauled round the capstan until the barge is brought up to its anchor, which is then picked up and rowed out again; and by this tedious process the barges would be dragged up all the rivers.

Even yet this system is not abandoned altogether, but it is fast giving place to steam-tugs or horse-power on the banks.

The barges are very large; many of not less than 50,000 poods (800 tons) burthen.

The manner of making arrangements for towing by horses is rather curious. The proprietors of the barges travel round to the villages in winter time, and bargain with whole villages, to supply a certain number of men and horses from each. Only enough men are kept at home to do the necessary work of haymaking and harvesting, and all the rest set out for the whole season to journey up the rivers with the barges. The pay is very poor; but the peasant is secured by a sum of hand-money down at the time of making the bargain, which enables him to be lazy and enjoy himself for a short time, until the early spring, when he sets out to work with the barges, and returns at the end of the campaign not one copeck richer than he was when he started. The inland carrying trade by barges and steamers is very profitable and much competed. It is not an unusual thing for a steamer to pay for herself in one year's work.

The steamers now are almost all Russian built; a good many large yards are established on all the principal rivers, and the quality of Russian iron being very good, some very good boats are turned out. As a rule they are not very highly finished, being only intended to be used as tug-boats; but they are not the less useful and profitable, and their numbers increase every year. All the shipbuilding yards on the internal rivers have their hands full of work, and new yards are now being set up on many of the rivers in Siberia. If the fleet of steamers on the Siberian rivers continues to increase as fast as that on the Russian rivers, the business will be immense.

The smaller rivers of Russia have an attribute which renders them more useful than those of warmer climates. It is this: although in summer they may not have water to float an ordinary barge, yet by the melting of the snow in the spring time, their waters are so much increased that they carry the largest and deepest laden barges on their stream; and it is surprising to see with what neatness and ease the peasants handle what appear to be unmanageable hulks. Freight by these barges is very cheap; the wood for building costs nothing, and the hire of the labourers is very small.

Goods can be sent from the Oural mountains to Nijny Novgorod, a distance of 2,000 versts, for 25s. per ton, including all the charges for shipment and delivery. The large rivers, such as the Volga and the Oka, are not so well maintained as they ought to be. The Government levy an *ad valorem* toll on all goods shipped on these rivers, of, I believe, a half per cent. This must amount to an immense annual sum; but in those parts of the river that I know best, I know that nothing has been done with this money for the good of the navigation, within the memory of the " oldest inhabitant."

The pretext for the tax is the maintenance of the navigation; but as nothing whatever is done to that end, the rivers are gradually getting choked up with sand-banks; and the Oka, one of the most important arteries of water-communication in the Empire, rising as it does in the government of Orel, and pouring into the Volga at Nijny Novgorod, used to be navigable for almost its whole course of

650 miles; but now, in summer time, it is in many places almost impassable, entirely for the want of a little dredging in season.

This matter, like many others, wants the attention of the heads of departments; subordinate officers exist, whose business it is, and who have received the funds to do all that is needful: what they have done with them is another question. An official of high position said to me, "I don't know where the money goes to, but I know it does not go into the Treasury."

Posting along the high roads (about 7,500 versts are kept up by the Government, and therefore in moderately good order), although not the most comfortable, nor the quickest, nor cheapest way of travelling, is yet arranged on the whole very well, and in a country of such vast extent as Russia can never become obsolete. The roads, it is true, are bad; this is the inevitable result of the great changes of the climate; the conveyances are built therefore with more regard to strength than easy motion; still, excepting at the season of the breaking up of the frost, and towards the end of the warm weather, it is no great hardship to travel in this way. In a good season of the year, one easily covers about 200 versts in twenty-four hours. The post-horses along the principal routes are nowadays better than they used to be, and the relays are ready at the stations; and in many other respects improvement is manifest, resulting from the increased number of travellers on the roads.

In the wildest parts it is perfectly safe to go unarmed; and all the stories that one reads of the necessity of revolvers, &c., are pure romance. Although I always carried a revolver as a matter of habit, in all my travelling in Russia, I never had more than one or two occasions to produce it, and would as soon go unarmed through the length and breadth of the Empire as I would through London streets. When we halted at a post-house for tea or any meal, we were accustomed to leave all our effects in the Tarentasse at the door, with nobody to look after them. There were wrappers, furs, and other articles lying about, but I never had anything stolen.

This absence of robbers, however, is only to be noticed in Russia proper. When I was travelling in Poland some years ago, my experience was of the contrary sort—there I lost two-thirds of my baggage by thieves before I got to the end of my journey, and I have heard other travellers complain of the same inconvenience.

The regular charge for post-horses on the Government road is three copecks a verst for each horse. As three horses are necessary, this is equivalent to fourpence halfpenny per mile, and there is a gratuity to be paid to the post-boy, of about sixpence for the stage of twenty versts, more or less. The carriage is called a "Tarentasse," a sufficiently commodious but cumbersome vehicle without springs, but mounted on the top of four or six long poles, which break the force of the jolting to a certain extent.

In Siberia, beyond Tiumen, the charge for horses is about half that of the Russian tariff. There the roads are very good, and it is possible to travel as much as 250 versts in a day's journey.

The expense of railway travelling is not much more than half of what it is in England. For example, the distance from Petersburg to Moscow is about 614 versts (425 miles), for which the first-class fare is nineteen roubles (or £2. 7s. 6d.), and for 5s. extra one gets a comfortable bed at night. The cars are built on the American model, and should rather be called luxurious than merely comfortable. Cards, chess, and dominoes are supplied on demand by the attendants, and, greatest luxury of all, the means of a good wash in the morning.

The centre of each car is fitted as a saloon, with velvet settees, a good fire, several tables, candles in sconces, a clock, and all that is usual in the furniture of a small drawing-room of the better sort.

Many of the stations have handsome refreshment-rooms, well supplied; but the long stoppages at these places are tedious.

The Russians have not yet learned the value of time, and do not understand our desire to push on expeditiously to the end of a journey. They generally think it necessary to be at their stations of departure about two hours before the train is to start. But a short time ago, at a station on the new line from Moscow, I found the peasants from a village close to the line, already waiting for their train, which was due six hours afterwards.

It is not remarkable that some of the Russian railways have not been well built, and there seems a difficulty in getting men capable to manage them properly. This is not astonishing, so many railways having been built at one time. All the lines are short of rolling-stock, and, in consequence, goods intended for forwarding, accumulate at all the termini. The old people of the anti-progress party point out this fact as a proof that the old methods of transport were better; but the great good that railways have already done, is apparent everywhere, and the extraordinary rise in the value of land is a great fact.

The authorities have taken up an excellent idea now that they have arranged the outlines of their network of railways, of making them serve intermediate districts better by the aid of a system of tramroads acting as feeders to the main lines. These can be laid down at a cost that will not devour the profits of the main lines as the costly branch lines of most of our English railways did.

It has been a practice in writing about the Russian railways, to describe most of them as merely military lines laid down for strategical purposes. This is, however, not their character. It is true that one or two may be said to be political roads, such as the line projected from Kiew to Warsaw, or the one from Kiew to Wilna, or from Samara to Orenburg, and the Caucasian railway. These, I believe, cannot yield any profitable return for many years; but I have no doubt—and nobody who has travelled the country and seen the riches of it, can have a doubt—that most of the other railways will be made to pay handsomely when their managers understand their business, and the rolling-stock is efficiently increased. They have one important circumstance in their favour—their cheapness.

Some years ago, the Englishman who had accepted the concession for the Sebastopol line, at the rate of over 100,000 roubles the verst, forfeited the caution-money rather than go on with the undertaking; but, now, many contractors would be glad to carry it out for less than half the price.

No doubt a great number of foreigners will be induced to travel about Russia now that the facilities for doing so are so great; and many among them will be men in search of profitable enterprise in the way of industry and commerce, of whom Russia has great need, and for whom she offers great opportunities just now. Such ideas were more in the mind of the great promoter of the new railway undertakings, than any of conveying troops from place to place.

It is easy to travel in Russia, even in ignorance of the language. The Russians are very quick at appreciating pantomime, and I am sure that anyone who wishes to travel through Russia and see for himself the wonders it contains, can, by the help of a Russian servant, get along perfectly well.

The system of telegraphs is now being rapidly extended, and the universal tariff system of sending messages is adopted. They are very well worked, as, for example, in out-of-the-way places in Siberia messages can be sent in French or German; and in many places even in English.

In the olden time travelling was not an easy affair in Russia, any small irregularity in a passport caused the unhappy bearer a host of trouble, as the following story will show:—

Two travellers, say X. and Y., arrived at the frontier station on the Petersburg-Berlin line, and were waiting to receive back their passports, which had been handed to the proper officials to be stamped, when the director of the department called and informed them that they could not leave Russia, as they had not got the permission of the police to do so. The travellers explained that they were ignorant of the formalities necessary, but having given the passports to the hotel-keeper and received them back again with some Russian writing inscribed thereon, naturally thought the matter was all right.

It was no use, the great man was implacable, and just as Y. had finally diplomatized the matter (which consisted in squaring the rouble question), X. upset the proposed settlement of the difficulty by exclaiming aloud, " Give him twenty-five roubles, he will let you go then ! "

The officer looked pleasantly at X., told the

travellers to fetch their baggage out of the train, and wait at the station until the train returned to St. Petersburg. They did not fetch their baggage out, but asked their fellow-travellers in the same carriage to look after it as far as the Prussian station, and if they did not arrive there before the train left to give their luggage to the Prussian station-master.

Finding out the train did not return to St. Petersburg until evening, Y., in the politest of tones, demanded permission of his excellency the aide to receive back the passports, as being hungry, they wished for breakfast, and thought it might be disagreeable walking about the town without these very necessary adjuncts. They were immediately handed over, and by this time the train could be seen safe over the frontier.

A help to the memory of a porter in the shape of a three rouble note, informed them that there was a small stream, which, if followed up half a verst in a certain field, could be easily crossed, and that this stream was the frontier. Our two disconsolate travellers therefore began to roam about, always towards the coveted point. When the semaphore telegraph between the station and guard-house went to work, the result of this "conversation" was soon visible in the flesh: two sturdy Cossacks, fully armed, commenced a march in the steps of the travellers, who by that time were following the bendings of the boundary stream, amusing themselves on the way by picking up stones, playing at hop-scotch, and other innocent devices, until the two warriors had fulfilled what were probably their orders of "marching up that river."

Having allowed the two soldiers to head them by some sixty yards, they jumped into and crossed the stream. On the opposite side the bank was a little high, and as X. and Y. were crawling up it on their stomachs the military arrived just opposite to them, and addressing our travellers in Russian (of which they understood nothing), made a great row. X. who was a more acquatic bird than Y., and therefore not so much disabled from the water and mud, ventured to look over his shoulder, and observed the warriors had their guns at the "present."

"Oh, you blackguards, you daren't shoot, we are in Prussia now."

This was no good. Y. then suggested as X. was the "banker" for the journey, "Why don't you throw them some money?"

"All very well talking," said X., "but how is a fellow to get his hand in his pocket when, if he moves, very likely he'll get a bullet in his —— " (well never mind where).

With a little engineering however he managed to extract a three rouble note, and wrapping a stone up in it, threw it over his shoulder across the stream (it was very narrow) to the implacable military.

Now the army were puzzled between looking wistfully at the fortune at their feet, and their officer, who was also watching the engagement from the look-out on the guardhouse; however, as I have remarked before, a Russian is generally up to an emergency (particularly if that should be a pecuniary one); one brother gives the other the order to march, and with his foot judiciously impels the covered stone.

A corner is soon reached which covers the view of the general on the look-out from his army, who then expressed to the weary and benumbed travellers that they had better be off as quickly as possible. The army returns to their discomfited commander and announce a defeat, and no doubt the general in charge has long since sent the umbrella which X.

lost in the engagement to the Kazan Cathedral, as a trophy of the brilliant victory of the army of Wirballen over the English. X. and Y. arrived at the Prussian station rather moist and muddy, in plenty of time for the train, and to take their hats off to his excellency the director.

Nowadays the difficulty is more easily got over. A year ago I was a fellow-voyager with an individual, dressed in the European fashion, with a great deal of very red beard and very little hair on his head; his luggage, he informed me, consisted of the small black bag in his hand, which contained a clean shirt and comb (he remarking, what is very probably the truth, that it is less inconvenience to purchase what you want where you stay, than to incommode yourself with luggage, which generally travellers find only goes to recruit the exhausted wardrobes of chambermaids and waiters), and a silk handkerchief full of oranges, which he was continually munching (he had no teeth). Arriving at the frontier it was found he had no permission either to go in or out of Russia on his passport, I therefore presume. he had come in *underground*, as there was an *underground* way into Serf-Russia, as there used to be an *underground* way out of Slave-America.

The director informed him he could not pass. In broken English he exclaimed, " I not pass? I'm a Pasha! Pasha not pass? that is very bad; I shall write to Constantinople," and immediately produced out of the black bag a large document with his titles all set out (as I suppose what he said was true, although nobody could understand the hieroglyphics on it). He could only speak a few words of English and a very little French. I tried to explain to him, that his passport was very much out of order,—but no, he was a Pasha, and could do as he liked.

I spoke to one of the many mercantile agents who are established there, and who are always obliging, and wishing to help a stranded foreigner, and he told me to direct the Pasha to the chief of the police, who, on an explanation of the circumstance would most likely let him pass. He galloped off to him, and arrived over the frontier, with the necessary permission, in time for the train. And as this circumstance happened some years after the former, I think it proves that travelling facilities have improved.

CHAPTER IX.

SIBERIA.

IF the other parts of Russia are comparatively unknown to foreigners, Siberia is still more so; and such remarkable ideas prevail in England about that country, that I am anxious as far as possible to correct them. I believe that to the minds of many people, the word "Siberia" conveys the idea of a vast frozen wilderness, inhabited only by political prisoners, whose life is passed in an unceasing struggle for the mastery with the bears who dispute the forest with them.

Let me try to correct some of these mistakes, by giving the result of my own observations.' First, then, as regards the climate. A country upwards of five thousand miles in length, by about two thousand three hundred in breadth, containing six millions of square miles of land and water, and calling among its boundaries such widely sundered names as the Arctic Ocean, the Sea of Japan, and Chinese Tartary, —extending thus: from latitude 45° 30′ to 77° 40′ N., and from longitude 52° 30′ to 190° E., must necessarily have great varieties of climate within its boundary line;—from Italian mildness in its most southern limits (about the same degree of latitude as Venice) to perpetual ice in the regions of the Arctic Ocean.

At Irkutsk, half-way to the Eastern frontier, near the great inland lake Baikal, which the Russians call the Holy Sea, the mean annual temperature is 31° Fahrenheit; and the mean temperature of the winter months is 1° below zero.

In the valley of the river Enisei (which empties its water into the Arctic Sea), owing to the shelter of the high land, very severe cold is unknown; and in the south towards the confines of the Altai mountains, cattle graze all the year round in the open air. In all this part of Siberia, then, south of 57½°, the air is very dry and the severity of the cold is not much felt; and it is in this latitute that the great bulk of the population are assembled, and here that the industry of the country is best exemplified.

At Ekaterienburg, near the Oural, I found very little, if any, difference between the climate and that of Moscow, which lies two degrees further south; while at Semipalatinsk, near the Altai mountains, in latitude 50° 40', or even anywhere south of Krasnoiyarsk, the climate is beautiful.

All about the southern parts of the Oural mountains is also healthy; and no fault can be found with the severity of the cold in any of those parts of Siberia that I am now discussing. The extreme northern or eastern latitudes are not desirable places to live in.

I travelled in many parts of Siberia, in which the climate was everywhere more or less temperate and endurable, never suffering myself from its severity, nor finding it anywhere worse than the climate of Moscow. A great deal of the land I saw to have a fine agricultural soil, a rich, deep black loam, where anything would flourish. The method of husbandry, however, must exhaust it very much, and could not be followed, if land were not plentiful and population scarce.

Year after year the crop of corn is the

same, with no manure, and much of it never lying fallow, and yet the crops are abundant enough to indicate the enormous production that might be worked out of the soil by a little intelligent industry. In the Oural mountains I saw maize that had ripened well in the open air, and some beetroot, and some potatoes which had grown to an extaordinary size.

In those parts of Siberia where the soil is less fertile, great quantities of rye are still grown, and a pood of rye-flour was quoted last year twenty copecks, or sevenpence for thirty-six English pounds.

The woods in the summer are beautiful; although the long days are hot, the evenings are always cool and rather damp; then the wild flowers grow everywhere in great luxuriance. Strawberries and raspberries, currants, cherries, and many other kinds of wild edible berries are gathered from the woods in great quantities, and sent off to supply the markets of neighbouring towns, which receive all their fruit from these wild growths.

The common necessaries of life are cheap here, more so than they are in other parts of Russia, where, however, they are cheap enough.

I obtained the following quotations, among others : beef, 2d., and veal, 1½d. the pound ; a goose, 12d. ; a large turkey, 2s. 6d. ; game of all kinds—birds, hares, &c., altogether at 1d. or 1½d. a head all round, without regard to size ; potatoes, 7d. the bushel ; oats, 3s. 9d. the tchetvert ; hay, 1¼d. the pood of thirty-six English pounds.

The roads in Siberia are as good as those of any part of the Empire, and, beyond Tiumen, they are better, and indeed equal to any ordinary post-roads in Europe. Travelling is, therefore, in that respect, not uncomfortable. The horses are celebrated for their speed. The posting-houses are tolerably good, much better than those of many parts of the centre of Russia, and in many of them it is possible even to get an eatable dinner. I was astonished at a post-house in one remote village, which was a model of cleanliness and comfort in other respects, to find this also: that the waiter offered me the selection of my dinner from a carte, supplemented by a list of wines of several varieties.

The peasants of Siberia are found to be far more civilized and better educated than those of the other parts of Russia. This is doubtless due to the influence of the political exiles who, from time to time have been sent from the centres of civilization to live among them, and many of whom, having no business to occupy them, spent their time in the charitable occupation of teaching the children of the peasantry of their neighbourhoods. There being less ignorance there is also less bigotry in religious matters. The churches are fewer in number, and, of course, the number of priests is also proportionately smaller. In Siberia, one is struck with the scarcity of churches, so different to the superfluity existing in other provinces of Russia.

The peasantry of Siberia are cleaner and better dressed, altogether a finer class of men than the peasants of other parts. They seem to talk and express their opinions with more freedom from restraint, and also to be better informed of what is passing in the the world than their countrymen of further south. Altogether they seem to have been more liberally educated and trained, and the traveller cannot fail to be struck with the improvement he must notice in the general condition and appearance of the people as he advances further north towards the Siberian deserts.

The rise of the scale of civilization in Siberia is indicated by the improved condition of the females of the population. In central Russia the woman is treated as all uncivilized people treat women, with neglect and tyranny. She is left to do the hard work and slave at field labour, while her lord and master alternates the amusement of drinking and sleeping.

The Mujik, in spite of his many amiable qualities, is decidedly reprehensible in his treatment of his womankind. Often in the glaring heat of a summer's day the women of the family may be seen toiling in the hayfield, with nothing on but their shifts, whilst the men are quietly taking a snooze sheltered from the sun under a house of green branches made for the purpose. Ask one of these lords of the creation if he is married, he may answer, "No, not yet; I am looking out for a good strong working girl, when I can find such a one that will work for me I shall marry, and not before."

Now in Siberia this evidence of barbarism is not so prominent. There the woman takes her proper place, looking after her household and her children, whilst the man attends to his proper duties also.

The finest town that I have seen in Siberia is Ekaterienburg, the frontier town between European and Asiatic Russia, a position which gives it many advantages, and in respect of which it possesses certain trading privileges. It is the chief centre of the government mining department, and is in near proximity to many valuable metallurgical undertakings, from which circumstances it derives much importance, and an increased population. Irkutsk is also a nice town, but Ekaterienburg has the superiority in several respects. It contains a population of 25,000 souls, and is handsomely built, possessing several fine churches, and a great number of brick and stone houses; among which some deserve to be called rather palaces, also a mint, and large mechanical works belonging to the Government. It has also a theatre, a club, and two really good hotels; and on the whole is as unlike a city on the outside borders of civilization and in the close neighbourhood of Asiatic barbarism as it is possible to imagine. I am sure that when eating the " dîner à la carte," supplied by M. Plotnikoff at the best hotel, I found myself as closely surrounded by the externals of civilization as I could be in any European city.

There is plenty of refined society to be met with in all Siberian towns, and the time of one's sojourn there always glides away pleasantly; the regularity and evenness of the climate being an addition to the enjoyment of life.

As to the inaccessibility of Siberia, the dangers, discomforts, and annoyances of the journey, its great expensiveness, and so on, the world has been much deluded by travellers' tales, and by the romantic imaginations of those who sympathise much with Siberian exiles.

Nijny Novgorod is now accessible enough, and has become quite a fashionable rendezvous during the great fair. From this place a line of steamers plies daily to Perm in Siberia, doing the distances pleasantly in a week. The boats are not large, and their accommodation must not be compared with that of the floating palaces of the P. and O. Company, but they are kept very clean, and cannot be called bad quarters for travellers.

Their provisions are plentiful and good,

and their tariff of charges is moderate. On the whole a very pleasant week may be spent by an observant man on this river journey. The few towns passed on the way break the monotony of the voyage, and the scenery is not without its peculiar recommendations; though I cannot endorse the opinion of those travellers who say that the river Kama, which we enter a short distance below Kazan, is splendid. Such eulogists must measure their admiration by a lower standard of beauty than I. Beyond Perm the journey is easy enough to any part of Siberia; it is certainly a little tedious, but even that depends in a great measure on a man's own resources for amusement, because there is plenty of pretty scenery, hill, wood, and water, which are a delightful compensation for a little jolting about, especially to a traveller from that flatter part of Russia, where even as much as a mole-hill upon the horizon is a natural curiosity, and the wearied eye looks round in vain for a relief to the everlasting monotony of the interminable sandy or grass grown steppe.

Excepting that small tract in the neighbourhood of the Oural mountains, which lies between the two watersheds of Europe and Asia,—say between Perm, in Europe, on the Kama, and Tiumen in Asia, on the Tura, near its junction with the Tobol; the rest of Siberia is intersected by a network of water communication in the great rivers Obe, Enisei, Irtish, Lena, and Amoor, navigable everywhere, and flowing through the country in all directions, and so connecting one end of Siberia with the other. If the small hiatus over the Oural passes, from Perm to the Tobol, were only connected by a rail, then goods would go from the extreme end of Russia in Europe all over Siberia by railways and water carriage.

All the chief towns of Siberia are connected by telegraph wires with the capital, and from thence messages are forwarded to all other telegraph stations in the world.

Looking at the map of Asia, at the short step from Irkutsk to the tea districts of China; at the navigable Amoor, so close to the wealth of Japan; carrying the eye down again to the Russian outposts near Cabul, and to those between the Black Sea and the Caspian, one is struck with the reflection that the development of Russia's system of internal communication would direct all Eastern trade from its existing channels, and perhaps place the city of Moscow at the centre of the carrying trade for the Eastern world. The resources of Siberia are immense. Few people have any idea of their importance. Her mineral wealth is almost unexplored; in the few places where it is worked it is so, most unsatisfactorily, and under the worst possible management. To judge of the importance of this part of the wealth of Russia, consider only the Oural mountains, which extend from north to south a distance of 1200 miles, and their slopes are known to contain more or less gold along the whole extent of them. Yet they are only worked in a few places, and there not as they ought to be. Consider, again, the large tract of copper producing country, and how few are the works scattered here and there upon it. And so it is with iron and all other minerals, they are all comparatively neglected. It is very saddening to travel through this country, and, knowing the stores of mineral wealth it contains, see its poverty and deplorable neglect of those stores.

Whenever I travel about Siberia, I always think why is it that our countrymen are sent all the way to the Antipodes in search of a colony. I speak of those who set out with a small capital in their pockets. Here, nearer home, they can get better land cheaper than in many of our colonies; they can live more cheaply, can hire labour cheaply, and enjoy many advantages of civilization which they would want in the colonies. While paying trifling taxes, or really no taxes at all, they would be under the watchful protection of the most paternal of governments, and in no danger of being devoured by wild Indians or Maories. And all these benefits against one drawback,— that of being settled in a country where the inhabitants speak another language, and the forms of government are of another nature than they have before been accustomed to. Again, an emigrant to the western prairies of America, or the sheep-runs of Australia or New Zealand, has no neighbours at all; but in Siberia he would have plenty, and among them quite a number who spoke several languages besides Russian. I know a small works hidden among the Altai mountains, where two at least among the workmen speak the English language.

Not only does farming here, but all other industrial enterprises likewise, offer a good occupation, and the promise of a fortune to a man who courageously and judiciously inaugurates and carries them through. In short, I can think of no other country in the world which offers the same advantages to a young man with a small capital as Siberia. I could give several examples of successful enterprise. It does not much matter what a man has been brought up for; if he only has a " head on his shoulders " he must get on, and that rapidly. Most of the merchants settled in Siberia are self-made men, in fact, there are very few who are not so. Such a man said to me a short time ago:—"Twenty years since, I came to this town with 800 roubles (£100), and I have made that into five millions; it is a good country to work in."

Siberia has begun to move forward a little, of late. To-day on her rivers may be seen thirty steamboats, exactly the same number that were on the Volga and Kama only seventeen years ago, and now on the Volga and Kama are 370.

Siberians build their own steamboats; they make rails, cloth, cotton goods, paper, &c.; they are much developing their carrying trade, and, year after year, navigating new rivers.

The Siberian aristocracy cherish two especial weaknesses: the first is, for playing cards; the other, for drinking champagne. As to card-playing, it is no longer an amusement to them — it is a serious business; and the Siberians are the most immoderate gamblers that I have ever known, even in Russia. In the hotel, in the room next to mine, four men sat down to play at 11 o'clock in the morning on Monday, and continued their game without interruption for sleep, but only now and again a few minutes' respite for refreshment, until the Thursday following! In the meantime, the individual who kept the bank had been cleared out with a loss of forty thousand roubles. At these settled and prolonged gambling orgies, one holds the bank against all the others, and the game is continued until either the bank is broke or the adversaries. What a picture of misery such a party must be about the third day! with blinking, blood-shot eyes and aching heads, trembling fingers and hands too weary to pick up the cards and money; propped up with cushions like so many paralytics, and kept alive by perpetual stimulants—one would find it a little more cheerful to be working with a pick at the bottom of the deepest mine in their neighbourhood.

At Irbit a great fair is held in February, which is largely attended by all the Siberian merchants, and here the gambling is universal and furious. A number of Jews and card-sharpers come to this fair from Kowno, Wilna, or even greater distances, in order to share in the immense plunder which changes hands at the card-tables on these occasions.

As at California and Australia, the fortunate gold-digger is the general victim of the gamblers, and, in one night, will clear out the whole gains of his gold expedition, and be sent off sobered and penniless on the following morning to dig again for more.

The sumptuary arrangements of the respectable residents in Siberia are made on a scale of extravagance and ostentation. As large incomes are earned, so large establishments are maintained, and hospitality is unbounded. The traveller from place to place, and among the Zavods, where no hotels exist, always drives immediately on his arrival to the "Gospotsky Dom," or gentleman's house, where he receives accommodation, as a matter of course, whether the proprietor of the house be at home or not.

On one of the steamboats between Nijny Novgorod and Perm, I had made a passing acquaintance with a gentleman who lived far up among the slopes of the Oural, where he combined the occupation of merchant and gold adventurer on a large scale, and he had pressed us to push our journey as far as his settlements, and come there and pay him a visit. One day, therefore, when I found myself passing at no great distance from his residence, I determined to make a short *détour*, that I might drink a cup of tea with this gentleman, and then push on further.

But I had reckoned without my host; as will be seen from the following story of my visit:—

We arrived at about seven in the evening, and our summons at the bell was answered by the appearance of a very old man dressed in the universal sheepskin, who I thought passed for the Dvornik, or house-porter. He demanded who we were, and our post-boy called out that we were two English princes! This was the result of an act of extravagance of my companion (who for the want of small change had given our previous post-boy 25 copecks instead of 5, which was his proper fee).

The old gentleman at the gate made a low salaam, and threw both gates of the porte cochère wide open. We crawled out of our Tarentasse, and followed him to the grand entrance of the house, where he left us to ourselves.

We found our way inside the house: our travelling friend at home, and a friendly welcome. So we were soon seated down to a glass of tea. I was describing the astonished appearance of the old Dvornik outside, and how he left us at the foot of the steps, when the door of the room was thrown open, and the same old gentleman, who acted Dvornik, of whom I was speaking, entered. He had discarded his sheepskin garment, and put on a magnificent Persian silk dressing-gown, and our friend introduced him to us as "My papa."

I may mention that "Papa" had been, in his generation, one of the most celebrated and successful merchants of those parts. Conversation went round pleasantly; but, after about two hours, we began to show signs of taking our leave; this was far from our host's intention. We must first have "Sarkuska" (Sarkuska is the ante-dinner, all sorts of dried fishes, hams, cheese, caviar, radishes, &c., with Schnapps of all sorts). Then a little sleep. On waking up, dinner was just ready at ten o'clock. More eating accordingly, and a deal more drinking, followed by cigars, as fine in flavour, said my companion, who had lived in Havana, as he had ever found in the West Indies.

Then it was too late for travelling further, so we went to bed. However, early on the following morning, I sent my servant to have the horses put to, that we might get away quickly, and make up for lost time. The servant came back with a message from the postmaster, that "We could not have any horses to-day." The fact being, that our host had forbidden him to forward our journey, that he might keep us a little longer the captives of his oriental hospitality. It was no use abusing the postmaster, he was too much afraid of our tyrannical host to do anything to offend him. We had to wait his appearance in patience. Presently he came down, dressed in full evening costume, as he had left us on the preceding night, and his father in similar gala apparel. I explained to him, with all appreciation of his hospitable intentions towards us, that nevertheless it was absolutely necessary for us to go forward at once. I wasted words, he would not listen to it; and we were obliged to spend another day in feasting and conversation, varied by the amusement of looking over the house, and admiring everything it contained, which was brought before us to admire, and fix a value on.

It is a very favourite amusement of such people to exhibit all their treasures to every stranger whom they entertain. We were fortunate enough to get released towards evening from the pressing, but unaffected, hospitality of our kind entertainers,—and the above is only one of a great many similar instances of hearty welcome and genuine hospitality for which I have been indebted to Siberian merchants.

The old gentleman ("my papa") who appeared to us first in the simple peasant's dress, was, until 1861, a serf; and yet, in 1869, I find him such as I have described.

His little grandson, ten years old, was getting a good education, and already spoke French.

His son, the active master of the business and household, was a very shrewd, well-informed man, who discoursed sensibly of the political parties in London and Paris, as well as at St. Petersburg, and who received his newspapers every day.

Where the extraordinary ideas come from concerning the prisoners and exiles in Siberia, I know not. There are two distinct classes of détenus : criminal prisoners and the political exiles, and these again are subdivided into several divisions.

First as to the criminal prisoners.

The worst culprits *only* are sent to work in the mines—mostly in the silver mines of the Nertchinsk district. As these are always the worst sort of criminals, guilty of murder, or other similar crime; and as the work in the mines is not particularly hard nor injurious to health, they may be considered to be a good deal better off than they deserve to; moreover, all the people working in the mines now live above ground.

Another class of criminals are those sent to various kinds of forced labour above ground.

And the remainder are only exiled to certain spots, where they are obliged to live under the surveillance of the police:

formed into little colonies among themselves, and I am told it is not advisable for strangers to pitch their tents among these colonies of criminals.

I have never heard any reason why the Russians should be said to treat their criminals worse than other nations. We hang our murderers; the French guillotine theirs; the Russians more wisely and humanely, in my opinion, use theirs for certain kinds of labour, and take the greatest care of their health. As an evidence that the prisoners are not enfeebled by their confinement, I may here note, that during these last months I have read of two escaped convicts taken at St. Petersburg, who had managed to tramp on foot all the way from Nertchinsk.

As to political offenders, they are subject to no further punishment than is involved in their compulsory residence within a certain distance of some given centre. So long as they do not go beyond their allotted circle, they are in all other respects perfectly free. Many among them have entered the employment of the Government, entirely of their own accord. Many of them also are now in a better position in Siberia than they would be in their own country, and have no wish to return home. Some, on the other hand, are in indifferent circumstances. One miner told me lately that in his works he was employing two men who had been colonels in the army, at eighty copecks a day for each. I do not believe that there is one instance of a political exile, properly so called, working in the mines, or doing any other kind of forced work for Government account.

It has been too common a custom to mix up some of the criminals with political prisoners in speaking of them. So you may hear that a certain prisoner is a " political," and, on going carefully into his case, you will find, that although the man may have been mixed up with politics in some way or other, yet he was sent to Siberia for some crime quite distinct from his political tendencies.

I am not only giving my own opinion, which, like that of other travellers, is very liable to error, but I am speaking the opinions of men educated and living on the spot, honest in their opinions, and well able to judge; and I think it only honest, as I have had unusual opportunities of collecting information on the subject, to record what I have heard and seen.

It is not my business to justify the act of banishing men from their homes, often for a mere expression of opinion. Their lot is doubtless unhappy enough, in the mere fact of their exile from all that is near or dear to them. It does not need to be painted in blacker colours than the truth will justify, nor exaggerated by false statements of cruelty and sufferings which do not exist.

Of late years, a great improvement has been made in the means of transporting prisoners of all kinds to their destinations. Formerly they walked on foot the whole distance, and months were consumed on the journey, and many fell victims to the fatigue. Now, steamers carry them to Perm, and from Perm they are sent on to their destination by carriages. So carefully are they looked after now, that in winter they do not travel on the roads. Five years is the shortest term of banishment. The worst kind of criminals have their heads shaved, some on one side only and some all over. I do not know the reason for this disfigurement.

Many prisoners make their escape, and find their way with comparative ease through the woods to the great towns. There they exist for a time, until they are found to be without passports, identified and returned to their punishment. These runaways, while hiding in the woods by day, come down to the villages at night to seek for something to eat; and so great is the goodness of heart of the Russian peasant, and his sympathy with anything like misfortune, that in many villages the peasants will every night leave food and drink outside the window of their cabins for these people to feed upon: although they know as well as possible that these may be some of the greatest villains upon the earth.

Never does one see in Russia a troop of prisoners clanking along the road or in the streets, without at the same time observing all sorts and classes of people giving them money and food. The Russian, particularly the peasant, has a very soft heart.

A curious variety of Tchinovniks is met

with in Siberia, as it is the head-quarters and centre of all metallurgical undertakings of the Government; it is full of the officers of the department of mines.

Amongst all Russian Government servants the mining engineers are the most intelligent and accomplished. Amongst the chiefs you find especially highly talented men, and men who are conscientiously trying to forward the interests of the Government in spite of the difficulties they have to struggle through. Among which inefficiency of their subordinates is the chief, but when the plan is carried on of transferring all these properties to private hands their development will be something very different to what it is now. Siberia, as I have said, is the important centre of Russia's mineral wealth, which it would be impossible to give an idea of within the limits of a chapter. There are gold, silver, copper, lead, iron, coal, and salt, and dense forests still undisturbed. I have travelled over miles of mineral wealth; for day after day through interminable woods; I have looked from the highest mountains, and from horizon to horizon, and seen nothing but thickly timbered forests covering the hills and valleys. All this is yet to be utilized, there it stands idle, as abundant as man can want, and only waiting for the axe of the emigrant, when the tide of colonization shall set towards Siberia, under the auspices of the liberal policy recently inaugurated by the Russian Government.

CHAPTER X.

THE GREAT FAIR OF NIJNY NOVGOROD.

NOTHING can give a stranger a better insight into the manners and peculiarities of the frontier population of Russia, than a visit to the great annual fair at Nijny Novgorod.

There Europe and Asia meet in harmony on the common ground of trade and mutual interests.

There the extreme eastern terminus of European railways is extended to the confluence of the great rivers, which bind the whole Empire of Russia in a net-work of water communication.

The fair begins some time in July, but it is at its most crowded and busy culmination from the 12th to the 28th of August (old style).

Let us leave the fair, cross the Oka and mount the hills at the back of the town; thence we can get a bird's-eye view of the fair, which is held about the angle where the Oka runs into the Volga.

It would have been impossible to select a better spot. On the Volga are barges which have sailed down the Kama from the Oural, laden with the produce of Siberia: iron, copper, lime-tree bark, rags, &c., and destined for the long journey to Astrakhan and the Caspian Sea, there to tranship their cargo to other vessels which will carry it to the ports of Persia. On the Oka are deep-laden barges destined to Moscow, or the centre of Russia, far away. Look at that barge seeming like a large merchant ship, it is freighted with 800 tons weight of corn for St. Petersburg. There is a strange Asiatic craft, curiously carved and coloured, and hung with extraordinary square banners, for it is a holiday and all the vessels are dressed with flags.

These big square banners are covered with devices in gold and silver and many colours, under the protection of whose cabalistic sentences the superstitious mariners sleep secure.

Watch the busy steamers, puffing in and out among the shipping, and looking dwarfed in the distance. There they all meet together, some from the gloomy regions of pine trees and snow in Siberia, some from the glowing borders of the Volga, where sandy deserts reflect the rays of dazzling sun.

The railway, type of the civilization of the West, stretches along the plains at our feet, and the representatives of Europe and Asia meet about its terminus to trade.

There are two barges passing one another, we can see from the gorgeous image of his favourite patron saint on the two flags that they belong to the same owner.

One of those barges contains tea from China; the other is laden with cloth goods and European notions addressed to the Chinese markets in return.

There is a barge towed by thirty horses, which is filled with petroleum from the Caucasus; another barge by its side is loaded deep with iron and copper from the Oural mountains.

Yonder, on the bridge of boats, which connects the town with the fair, is a heavy lumbering Tarentasse drawn by six horses, and escorted by a light cloud of very irregular cavalry, Cossacks, riding with their chins on their knees, and their long lances in various angles in the air.

That banditti-looking body-guard suggest a *quis custodiet custodes?* The carriage contains gold washed in the Altai mountains, and now on its way to the mint at St. Petersburg to be coined. A dusty and much enduring officer in charge has made the interior of the carriage into as comfortable a bedroom as circumstances would permit; and must have found out, by concussion, every knob and angle of his compartment in the course of his unbroken journey of about six weeks.

Another carriage is crossing the bridge; an open one this time. What lord of creation sits so pleasantly alone on the back seat, puffing his cigar?

A countryman of our own evidently, for in addition to his umbrella spread, there is on his knees the inevitable red-bound handbook.

That cigar will bring him into trouble. See! I thought as much! His Isvostchick suddenly gallops as hard as he can make his horses go. A Cossack is after him! Another! The deluded Briton looks round and smiles on his escort of Cossacks. He thinks it is a compliment. It will cost him a fine of 25 s. r. for breaking the regulation against smoking on the bridge and in the fair.

That row of small wooden huts painted blue, which seems to be pitched in the middle of the river, is built in effect upon a sand-bank in the Oka, which with the most accommodating and convenient regularity, always appears above the water in time for the annual fair, although it is hidden beneath the surface in the winter and spring.

It is called the Siberian or Iron line.

The immense piles of iron that we see, and the contents of those other barges, now unloading the freight they have brought from the north, and of many more barges to follow, will be sold and sent away during the fair. Already there are a number of barges loading for the south; and so important is this part of the trade that the railway is brought across the water by a temporary bridge, right into the centre of this insular hive of industry. In a few months the sandbank will again be hidden by the waters, and not a mark will remain to record the passing importance of the ground that they cover.

Still, taking advantage of our commanding point of view (on the hill before mentioned), we can form an idea of the plan upon which the permanent part of the fair, the fair proper, has been built.

Yonder regular-shaped, bazaar-looking place, with its radiating alleys or streets, was originally sufficient for the itinerant merchants who frequented it, and year by year it has been increased round the same centre. The large house in the very centre (like the spider in the middle of his web) is the palace of the governor-general of the place. The governor resides permanently in the upper town, and only here during the fair.

The approach to it from the back contrasts with the narrow passages of the fair. It must be a pleasant escape from the dust and heat of the crowds, to emerge into that handsome broad boulevard with the shady trees. The boulevard ends in a handsome church. There is a smaller church, a great favourite with the people, built just opposite the governor's house, and facing the river; that little church the merchants of the fair built, to commemorate the Czar's escape from the dastardly attempt that was made on his life in April, 1866.

On each side of the chapel is a flag, of Chinese appearance; these two flags indicate the continuance of the great fair, and are hoisted with many ceremonies at its commencement, and remain floating until its close.

Looking now beyond the fair to the banks of the Volga, you may see some small brown mountains on the shore. Some of these are rags from Siberia, others the bark of the lime-tree, used for making what we in England call bass mats. Near them is an enormous heap of grindstones from the Oural, enough to serve the magic mill that grinds the salt for the sea; but all those tons of millstones will be shipped away to-morrow, and another quantity piled in their places.

The Exchange is yonder wooden-building with a blue-painted roof, near the other side of the bridge; of the great crowd of men congregated there, nearly all are owners of the various craft ready to be chartered for the Oural mountains or the Caspian Sea, St.

Petersburg, or Astrakhan (where you will), along the silent highways that are the main arteries of the Empire's life and strength. These are the men to carry your purchases home for you; their barks are on the shore, and the traktir is handy, where you may clench your bargains over a glass of tea.

It is worth while now to look round for the signs of manufacturing industry and progress. At some distance on the right you will see a ship-building yard; that is Kolschin's. He has a great many boats in hand, and has just laid the keels of three steam-vessels, which will be plying next year on the Tobol in Siberia.

On the other side of the Oka, just above the fair, you may notice a large red-brick building with a tall chimney; that is a saw-mill hard at work cutting planks, which will be made into railway waggons. Higher up you see larger works, with a deal of fire coming out of the chimneys; that is a large blistered steel works. Its owner is a leviathan in trade, who has a capital of ten millions of roubles, but who is so very stingy in small matters, that, if you receive a letter from him in answer to yours, you will see that he has turned your own envelope inside out, to use again.

When we have taken thus a bird's-eye view of the fair, we will come down from our point of vantage and plunge into the thick of it at once. In the crowd the dust is horrible, and the heat of the sun very oppressive.

It is the 15th of August, the day on which the business of the fair reaches its greatest importance, when the excitement is at fever height; finally the day when all outstanding drafts must be honoured.

The fair has a singular appearance from the immense quantities of goods which are piled up in store outside the shops, and covered up in mats to protect them from the possibility of damage from rain; for it does occasionally rain here copiously, and then the streets are more than ankle-deep in floating mud, which has its *désagrément*, but is preferable to their present condition, by which we are blinded in clouds of fine dust.

There is a part of the fair where almost all the goods are Russian produce; among them, those many-coloured trunks with metal bindings, are an institution of the country, and every peasant, man and woman, aims at the independent possession of such a chest, in which he can store away his little " all," and still have room for more.

Those copper and polished urns for making tea are called " Samovars." They come from Tula, on the Oka, not far from

Moscow, along with the comical intricate padlocks, by their side; a Russian loves a trick, or an artful dodge in everything, and despises a plain, straightforward padlock, with an ordinary key, so these are made to suit his taste; many of them require one or two springs to be touched before the key-hole is visible; others have a visible key-hole which will not admit the key until the hole has been moved by a spring. The generality of the Russian padlocks have a screw for a key, the worm of which is so made as only to fit its particular lock.

Here are carpets made of long coarse wool from Siberia, altogether peculiar in material and pattern. They are generally used by the better class of peasants to hang over the backs of their sledges, and are quite a Russian manufacture, although I have seen one hanging outside a shop in London with the label, "Persian rugs," which I recognized as one of a parcel which I had sent home from Nijny Novgorod, and which had been made at Tiumen in Siberia.

You are astonished at the neatness of the patterns of those wall-papers; it seem to be a manufacture for which the Russians have a very pretty taste.

That thick hairy-looking stuff which yonder native of little Russia is cheapening, is called "Voilok." It is a felt, made of cow's hair, compressed, and is a very useful article to a Russian. Amongst other purposes a sheet of "Voilok" is everywhere the peasants *bed*, and of this he also makes his winter boots.

As we are now in his house and informed he is at home, let us go and pay our respects to the governor.

While our names are taken in, we are ushered into an ante-room already full of officials, who are waiting to be summoned in rotation to their interviews with the great man. These officers are all in court costume, with cocked hats and swords, and wear all the orders they possess. Among them are some uniforms that probably seldom see the light of day, and whose wearers are uncomfortable scarecrows in their unaccustomed finery. I see by my side one such character, whose features are distorted into an unalterable smile, that would be symptomatic of downright idiocy, if it were not equally attributable to nervousness and discomfort. He seems to be dressed in the cast-off and worn-out uniform of a Cabinet Minister, which fits him much too tightly across the chest. He has a cocked hat under his arm, and a court sword between his legs. His darned and shining kid gloves smell of turpentine afar, and even these are too tight for him. Altogether he is so strapped up and strapped down, and starched and pomaded, that he looks as if he could not wink without bursting his buttons. He is the procureur of a small country town, and is waiting to consult his excellency about an "affair." I had seen this official a short time before on "business," when his costume (civilian) and the way he did his business reminded me of Hampton Races, and the thimble-riggers there. This man's evident tremor of nervousness gives my friend a wrong opinion of the governor, which is soon set right when I introduce him to a jolly-looking, middle-aged general, beaming with good humour and kindness, who chats agreeably with us for a long time; tells us all the news of the fair, and gives my English friend a high opinion of the Russian officials.

His virtues are not confined to the amenities of social life, but he is active and efficient, and honest in his government also.

If all the provincial governors in Russia resembled General O—— in these respects, things would go on much better than they do now. We take our leave and return to the scene outside.

The basement of the governor's house is arranged as a bazaar, divided into stalls occupied by specimens in an ethnological museum. First, we come to a counter stocked with old familiar Swiss chalets, churches, chamois, goats, and other objects carved in horn from Switzerland. The Teutonic proprietor recommends his wares in the patois of the Oberland.

In the next stall a bearded disciple of the false prophet, a native of Bokhara sits in silent state among silks, Cashmeres, scarves, and other Indian haberdashery.

Opposite to him is an eager, vulture-featured Tartar, who has brought turquoises from Persia; next, a gigantic Russian from

Ekaterienburg, in Siberia, a leviathan in enterprise as well as in stature, with a valuable store of precious stones; by his side a delicate-featured and long-haired Circassian, in the picturesque costume of his country, with a store of silver filagree work; then a fire-worshipper from Shiraz, with a display of Persian carpets of his own manufacture; a Parisian with kid gloves from Paris; a *soi-disant* Englishman, with a shop full of German toys; a spectacle-maker and optician from Berlin: and so round the bazaar, with a new nationality represented in every stall we approach.

And all these people are busily at work, lying hard in each other's faces, and trying to cheat the public. Your haberdasher from Bokhara keeps his Persian silks beneath the counter, until he has tried to sell you Moscow made counterfeits. Your Circassian, for his silver filagree work, has imitation ware of Tula, which is not so durable nor so costly as his own; and the pious and dignified Persian has carpets to sell to the uninitiated, which do not carry the leaden stamp of the Custom House, by which all genuine foreign goods are distinguished. In brief, they are all rogues alike, and he who would deal in the fair must have a sharp eye, or a good knowledge of his goods, or a resignation to submit to a certain amount of fraud.

"Well, well," I hear my reader exclaim, as he buttons up his pocket again with a tolerant smile, "it is worth being cheated of a few pounds to have dealings with the representatives of so many great nations assembled in one great exchange."

It is cruel to destroy the illusion, but I must now do so.

The interesting beauty from Circassia is an Armenian merchant, well known and indigenous at St. Petersburg. The true believer is a native of Nijny Novgorod itself. The Tartar with the turquoises, whose savage features suggested an existence of perpetual danger or violence, is a peaceable citizen of Moscow, who keeps a small shop in the Gostinoi Dvor of that city. But my Siberian giant is better than some of his precious stones; he is no sham, as I have seen him in Siberia, where, it is to be supposed, he also picks up his stones for sale.

The carpet manufacturer, also, is a genuine personage; a great merchant in his own line of trade; a man of education. I suggested to him that he would sell his Persian carpets better in London than here. "Yes," he said, "I send plenty to London; but for thirty-five years my family have attended the fair, and we don't like to give it up. It is a holiday, and we see the world, and know what is going on; the trade we do here does not pay us, but we should not like to give it up." (He did not say anything about *those carpets* that have no *leaden seal* of the Custom House; perhaps they pay expenses better than the legitimate trade). However, he is very polite, and as I have never in my previous visits made the acquaintance personally of them, I express a wish to see the interiors of the Persian line. He formally makes me known to a coterie of grave and courteous gentlemen in high black caps, saying that I am a Christian, but one who has no disrespectful intentions towards themselves; and so returns to his occupations, which I interrupted, of smoking cigarettes, and winding his long moustachio gracefully round the forefingers of his hands.

The Persian "notions" are silk, fruits, and carpets from Persia in great number and variety; rugs of long wool from the

Caucasus; drugs from Central Asia; gorgeously embroidered slippers from Teheran; shawl-patterned dressing gowns of warm and vivid colour from Meshed; turquoises from the neighbourhood of Herat. All the goods in this line appear to be genuine articles, but of very wide range as to quality. The Persians do not bargain and chaffer about prices like a Russian dealer; their form of swindling tampers with the *quality* of their goods rather than with the price. For example, I took up a roll of red silk, the price of which I was told was twenty-five copecks the arshine (tenpence a yard), and on looking inside it, I discovered that the silk became thin by degrees and beautifully less as it wound towards the centre; so that from a moderately thick web on the external layer, it gradually dwindled to a mere transparency of muslin. When I diffidently called the attention of the very gentlemanly dealer to this arrangement, he shrugged his shoulders, and replied indifferently: "What can you expect for twenty-five copecks the arshine?"

The furniture of all their private rooms is alike and simple enough; a raised bench for a divan, with plenty of cushions and carpets, are all that they require.

Let us now leave these Persians, and turn into the "line" that is frequented by the Bokhara traders. We are arrested at the first counter by an exhibition that would make the fortune of any wax-work establishment in the world.

Five Bokharians of distinction sit cross-legged on the counter, in front of a cotton store, in the form of a crescent; they have fine manly countenances, copper or snuff-coloured skin and jet black hair, and their quick, sharp, black eyes leap forward, flashing to meet you. All five were handsomely hung in robes of silk, with lots of jewellery; but the chief who sat in the centre was distinguished by a Caftan of many colours, and a silver girdle round his waist, which was literally overloaded with precious stones, principally turquoises. Their attention was evidently concentrated on the beauty of their own personal appearance to the detriment of their business. I asked the old image in the centre how much he wanted for a piece of silk that hung for sale behind him, and I was rewarded by a magnificent stare out of ten beady black eyes,—but all the five traders disdained to reply. Afterwards, a servant came forward and explained to me that those great lords in the fine clothes were in the wholesale line of business, and the silk trade was a retail speculation of himself—their servant.

These gentlemen had come to Nijny in their finest clothes, to sell a crop of cotton and carry back sheet iron in exchange. If they had only set up a wholesale trade in their own photographs, I would like to be their agent for London and Paris, at a low rate of commission.

To the left of the Bokharian line is a row of shops, full of the Russian speciality called " Tissues," fabrics of gold and silver thread, or woven in various colours, and used for the vestments of the priests, and the ornaments of the churches; also finer and lighter fabrics, which are exported all over the East, and most largely to Persia, to make the ladies trousers of.

There is a Tartar line, full of manycoloured leather boots, slippers, &c. One of the dealers objected to sell me a pair of what he called " Mosque slippers," "because," he said, " I never went to the Mosque, and therefore did not want them." It took a little perseverance to convince him that that was my business and not his.

Here also we find a great miscellaneous collection of Oriental and Russian produce of every kind; caviar, rhubarb, isinglass, betel nuts, a list too long to glance at of Russian manufactures, nick-nacks without end, from Paris and London, of every kind, and of the newest as well as of the older inventions; in fact, almost anything saleable that the mind of a merchant can conceive, and a great deal more than he could discover any quotation for in a trade circular, is here offered for sale.

The business transacted is genuine and immense; quickly done too, and without unnecessary chaffering.

Among the merchants of the Siberian line is a gentleman with whom I had much business, and who has honoured me with an invitation to dinner. Although his transactions at Nijny are carried on in only a very small shed of a place, one of the blue-topped ones I have described, yet he is actually one of the richest and most enterprising merchants of Russia, who, with twenty million roubles of capital, trades from one end of the Empire to the other; and answers those, who inquire of him where he has agents, with the magnificent reply, "In every town between Archangel and Astrakhan."

His dinner party is a reunion of many of the leading merchants of Russia, and owners and managers of many great industrial undertakings. Altogether, I calculate, that properties covering more than five millions of acres were represented at that table.

Among the company sat one fine patriarchal old gentleman who had a long white beard. He had formerly been the coachman of the founder of the firm, the father of his host; but now for thirty-five years had been aide-de-camp and chief manager in the business. He belongs to what is called the *Old Faith*. He is considered to have been one of the shrewdest hands at a bargain, in the Empire; and has a cunning habit, very prevalent among his class, of assuming *deafness* when he is engaged on matters of business, so as to get more time to consider his answers to the questions, he troubles you to bawl into his ears. However, once on a railway, I whispered very softly to him,—

"Michael Michaelovitch, let us have a glass of tea!"

"Come on," he answered, without a symptom of deafness.

He is a tea-drinker who would astonish anybody. I have seen him take twenty tumblers of tea at a sitting, and feel no bad effects from it.

The dinner was well chosen and well cooked. Our host's kitchen was in the hands of a chef from Paris, and no luxury that Nijny, Moscow, or Petersburg could supply, was absent from the repast; and this I must add, was not considered an exceptional festivity, but a dinner of daily routine during the fair, when open house is the rule, and perpetual feasting the custom, among all who are connected by any ties of trade.

After dinner we paid a flying visit to the Pagodas of the so-called Chinese line; where however we found no celestials, but veritable Mujiks and their masters from Moscow.

A number of bald-headed Tartars were about the streets, who looked like shaven maniacs as they grimaced at each other vehemently in conversation.

We looked in at the theatre as we passed. It is a decently built house, poorly attended, where we saw a scene from the Russian translation of Shakespeare's Hamlet; pronounced there "Gamlet," there being no aspirate in the Russian language, its duty is always overdone by the letter G.

There is better fun in Nijny than the half empty theatre. The traktirs are all crowded and full of life; we selected that called Barbadienkoes, where the real Zingari perform.

The room was crowded with many ranks of people, but among them scarcely any uniforms of civil or military officers.

In the capitals of Russia, there are more Government employés than civilians at all public places of entertainment; but at the great fair of Nijny commerce reigns supreme.

Rough-looking, bearded merchants were consuming champagne like water, nothing but champagne or tea was on the tables. As our friends at other tables became aware of our presence, glasses of wine were brought to us from various Ivans and Michaels, who were holding up their own glasses to catch our eye and challenge us. This custom of sending a glass of champagne to a friend while you drink his health, is prevalent through *all* ranks of Russian merchant society.

The guests were already noisy and talkative enough, but there were not many drunk yet. That would come.

Now silence for the gipsies, who were taking their places on the stage.

They arranged themselves in two half-circles; the women sitting in front on chairs, and the men standing behind. The leader of the band took his place in the centre, with a guitar.

The women were gaudily dressed in bright colours, wearing many ornaments. Their beauty has been often celebrated, and, I think, deservedly. They resemble in features the English type, but stamped with more intellect and refinement.

The older women of the party, however, had lost that delicacy of outline by which the younger ones were distinguished. Among the men I was struck with their resemblance to Jews.

When the audience was hushed with expectation, the leader gave a signal by jerking his arm and guitar, and one of the women broke out into a low, plaintive song, which elicited a shout of admiration from the audience.

She sang quietly and without effort, her bright black eyes wandering to all the corners of the room meanwhile; and, it may be, the *furore* with which her song was received, was as much due to the fascination of her glancing eyes, as to the music of her song. I saw the same woman sing the same song once again, at an entertainment which the merchants of the fair gave to the Grand Duke Vladimir, and her success then was as great, or greater.

She was followed by a chorus, in which the whole band joined; and the vehemence with which this was performed by all of them, was a great contrast to the plaintive tranquillity of her previous solo. The performers worked themselves up to frenzy pitch, shouting, hallooing, snapping the fingers, setting the whole body in a quivering motion, as the Eastern dancing girls are taught to do; while the leader with the guitar, who was a neatly built, little man, kept revolving on a pivot most gracefully in time to the music, his little black eyes flashing on each part of the room as he gyrated. Altogether, we were a good deal astonished at the gipsy performance.

Some ethnographical student would do

well to study the gipsies in Russia, as there is certainly more than one class of them. Nothing extraordinary is found in the type of the majority of those generally met with in the neighbourhood of the large cities, such as Moscow and Kazan; the women being much of the race found in other countries, and the men with a strong Jewish resemblance, particularly to the Karaim Jews, who principally live in the Crimea. But in travelling about, I have sometimes met with quite a distinct class, much darker in colour, longer curling jet-black hair, thick lips, and straight nose; in fact, a very Egyptian type of countenance. I have found this class decidedly less fond of gay dresses than most of the tribes, and a more working people than the generality of gipsies.

I met such a tribe once on the road, the other side of the Oural mountains, and I noticed a great peculiarity in their women, some thirty or forty; their dresses were all alike, old and young wore the same dark-coloured material, with long cloaks also uniform in colour, and apparently of some sort of cloth; but more curious still, these cloaks were all fastened with brooches alike, and made of a circle of copper as large as small tea-cups. This singularity of dress was so striking, that in the distance I had mistaken them for some prisoners on the march, and sent the Starosta from the post-house (where we were changing our horses) to give them some copper money. I shall not easily forget the sequel. The gipsies literally tore the poor fellow's clothes to pieces, to get the copecks, and would not believe in the emptiness of his pockets when he had scattered the money he had in his hands, which he was glad to do to escape from their clutches. Some of the younger of the women were passing beautiful, but the older were veritable hags. Their pertinacity in begging was astonishing, but in that even they differed from the regular gipsies; they did not try the usual plaintive whining or fortune-telling style, but boldly asked for what they wanted.

On another occasion I observed the same peculiarity as regards sameness of dress. This may be, perhaps, a type of the original gipsy that, according to Grellmann, came from Hindustan. It is no doubt true, from my observation, that this particular type of the race is to be found in those parts of Russia bordering upon Central Asia; and in support of Grellmann's supposition, it is a fact, that the gipsies I have alluded to do not speak the Russian language correctly, although they must have had four centuries in which to acquire it. The manners and customs of these gipsies without doubt assimilate in many respects to those of the Indians; but, on the other side of the question, the fact must not be lost sight of that these tribes, in common with all others, designate their chief as "Waywode," derived no doubt from the Sclavonic. It is very observable of all the Russian dancing gipsies, that although as elegant in their movements as their compeers in other parts of the world, they are decidedly not nearly so lascivious in their movements.

We went next to a remote corner of the fair, or rather, I should say, to an adjacent village beyond the town, to see the tipsy people wallowing in a barbarous scene of debauchery and degradation. Their orgies are beyond all description, and those who know most of them say,—

"There is no viler hell upon earth than Nijny Novgorod, in the fair time, for those who choose to make it so."

Returning to the more decent amusements

of the fair, we entered another traktir, where the national dance of Russia was being performed in appropriate costume. This costume consists of red skirts, black velvet knickerbockers, and polished boots, and a felt cap on the head, very much like the flat cap worn by the Beefeaters at the Tower of London.

The dancers were mostly boys and young men, and the dance, performed squatting on the haunches, with the arms a-kimbo, must be a violent muscular effort, much more athletic than graceful. This entertainment is very much patronized by your genuine Russian of whatever rank, and among the company was a large proportion of highly respectable and very solvent merchants. Among them I found an acquaintance, a well-dressed and quiet-looking young man, but who was drinking as much as was bad for him, and sending glasses of champagne to all comers. Before him on a table stood in a row at least a dozen bottles of Rœderer; he had two waiters attached to his especial service, and they were dressed, not in cotton, like the other waiters in the room, but in Persian silk. This extravagant young gentleman is one Karl Karlovitch, the only son and partner of one of the largest tallow merchants in distant Siberia. He was just twenty-two, and had come down to Nijny on business, to sell a quantity of tallow, and, as he called it, to "see the world," which, being interpreted, appears to signify, to make a tipsy fool of himself, and distribute his father's commercial capital among the hotel-keepers and worse characters of Nijny.

The story of the gross of green spectacles is eclipsed by his exploit at this present fair as I heard some time afterwards. His confiding parent and partner had the incalculable rashness to entrust this young man with tallow to the value of £25,000 sterling, and, as if the boy's natural propensities were not in danger enough among the temptations of the fair, and in the possession of such a sum of money, he charged him to be very particular about the sale of the tallow, and to keep all his papers in order; and, when his business was done, to enjoy himself at the fair before returning. This, I am told, is a common ordeal for the Russian youth entering manhood; the idea being that after one wild and unrestrained debauch he is likely to settle down sickened to a quiet life in his native town.

On these occasions very large sums of money are frequently squandered; often as much as £5,000 sterling in a short time; but Karl Karlovitch punished his father more severely still.

He arrived home in due time, and was

immediately called on for his accounts, which he produced in perfect order, and all very satisfactory. Thereupon the old man praised his son, and asked for the money.

"As to that," said Karl Karlovitch, "I have not brought home any money; I have spent every copeck at Nijny." And so he had; it had all melted away in amusements.

Since then, I hear, he has become wiser, and is now considered one of the steadiest and cleverest merchants of Siberia.

Another young merchant of my acquaintance was in that traktir. He was a much more modest youth of the type of the old school of Russian merchants, also from Siberia. His mother asked me if I thought a visit to London would do the dear youth any good; and I strongly recommended it, as calculated to enlarge his views of the world and society. Accordingly he came, and I happened to be in London myself when he arrived; so I met him at the London-bridge Station, and took him at once to the midst of the crowds.

Here he was so utterly astonished and frightened, that he could do nothing but cross himself continually. At last he said to me, "Would you believe that my poor dear old mother told me that Moscow was a much greater place than London!"

The visit to the last traktir ended our day's amusement, and we retired to bed. A few years ago there was not a decent hotel in the town; now there are two, "The Hotel Post" and "Soboleff's," which are both very clean and comfortable. Those who have travelled much in Russia know how to appreciate a comfortable bed and clean, free from the bugs and fleas which abound in most Russian hostelries.

Next morning being a beautifully bright day, we took a stroll on the river side, among the Tártars and Mujiks at work, loading and unloading the craft. They all work peacefully and cheerily together, nearly all singing, and are as happy over their work as so many children at play. Brawling or fighting are not seen; they do not work very hard nor very steadily.

Here is a party of Russians from our own province of Tambov unloading a barge commanded by one of our peasants. We will go on board and shake hands with him, by which he will see the difference between a Russian and a foreign master. Your Russian owner would about as soon think of shaking hands with a peasant as he would of walking half a mile afoot, which is the strongest improbability I can bring to compare.

Meanwhile the crew have knocked off work for their breakfast; they all stand round in a ring, take their hats off, and ask a blessing, crossing themselves at least ten times;

after which, they all sit down round a great wooden bowl of soup. Then the foreman hands each a lump of black bread, and a wooden spoon is placed before each, some salt is on the deck before them, which they sprinkle on their pieces of bread; then the foreman takes a spoonful from the bowl and lays his spoon down again; each of the others follows in regular order, laying his spoon on the deck as soon as he has swallowed his soup. So they go on quietly until the bowl is empty, when they all rise together, say another prayer, crossing themselves, put on their caps, and are ready for work. This decency of behaviour at their meals, and the manner of them, is another very oriental trait in the character of the Russian peasantry.

We just peep on board the steamer starting for the Don. The *table d'hôte* is laid with a clean white cloth, and shining plate and glasses for luncheon, and the waiters standing round in their clean cotton dresses, carry as fine a polish as the mahogany fixings of the sofas.

We return to the fair and try our hand at "catching a Tartar."

"How much for these skins, Ivan?"

"Twenty roubles."

"Twenty roubles! Why you must be a robber to ask such a price!"

"By G—d they cost me eighteen roubles."

"I'll give you five."

"Now, Barrin, you are laughing at me; but there, I'll take fifteen roubles!" (more swearing) "They cost me thirteen."

"Now, I'll give you ten roubles. Not a copeck more!"

Well, I get them, rather suddenly at this price, and think them certainly a bargain, until Ivan has safely pouched his money, when he offers me twenty more of the same sort for eight roubles; and, as I reject this, he finally says I shall have them for five. Then I begin to doubt whether the skins are worth anything at all.

However, I have bought them, and the next step is to have them properly packed and sent to my inn; no difficulty in this. A Tartar has his eye on me already. He is one of a guild of artizans whose trade it is to pack; and very well indeed they do it, in the open street in front of the shop.

Here are some curious little brown cakes of a substance like asphalte. They are what is called "brick tea," a favourite beverage of the Calmucks and Tartars, who make it into soup by boiling it in a pot with mutton, fat, onions, &c. When it is cooked they pour it into a bowl, and drink it with wooden spoons.

We meet a great number of Armenians all over the place. They are the Jews of the

East; awful men to drive a close bargain; but a wonderfully industrious people. All the embroidery work that is so plentiful in the bazaar is the work of the women of the Armenian provinces of the Caucasus.

It is very striking to see what polite, well-informed, and gentlemanly men the Persians are. If their nation is fairly represented in the fair they must be a highly polished race.

In a silk shop a Mujik merchant is buying a dress for his wife and calls us to counsel him. This is an important business; the dress is probably meant to last the lady's life, and to be transmitted as an heirloom to her descendants. He is hesitating over a yellow moire antique; but he cannot understand the name of the stuff, and asks me to tell him what it is. I tell him that it is an English manufacture, which settles him at once. He buys it.

In the meantime an old woman is bargaining for a silk handkerchief for her headdress. She has fixed the price of one which for colour is something like a rainbow broken up in a kaleidoscope. But still she asks the patient dealer, for a pattern with more colours in it. The shopman, who is a quiet wag in his way, answers very earnestly, "There are no other colours invented but those which are in the handkerchief."

Turning into the (*par excellence*) restaurant of the fair, where Nikite Egoroff dispenses everything that is good; all that is in, and all that is out of season; we order a pheasant for lunch, and take our places at a window looking into the poultry yard. In a moment we see our waiter and others in full chase of the pheasants: from which we conclude that ours will not be likely to be well hung, but the chase is a long one, and we hope the exercise will make him tender.

Meantime we overhear much interesting

comment on the dealings of the fair. How P. has bought three millions poods of iron; that Bokhara cotton won't sell; that tea is dearer; and that the Russians still stick to the caravan tea, in preference to all sea-borne sorts; several new railways, we hear, have been concessionized; money is cheap; trade generally good, and Russia prospering.

After lunch, a cigar in the sewers. All smoking is prohibited in the fair, but the sewers are arranged in regular streets, lofty and ventilated, entered by small round towers, with staircases built at intervals, flushed regularly, and on the whole kept very clean. Here the Mujik descends to enjoy the weed forbidden in upper day, and while he enjoys himself, fumigates an objectionable atmosphere. Our curiosity in the sewers was exhausted sooner than our first cigar.

We emerge near a money-changers; the booths of these men are of eastern appearance, open in front; they are doing a great business, and the amount of coin and money in circulation in the fair must be immense. All these money-changers are either Armenians or men of the old faith, and of the detestable sect called Scoptsi. They are, however, generally honest in their dealings; although, I am told, they are always ready to give a certain price for forged paper money, which I believe they sell again as a forgery.

The military band is playing at the back of the governor's house, and we sit for a moment on a bench to watch the evening promenade on the boulevards. Here we see the more idle sort of visitors to the fair, sunning or airing themselves, generally walking in small parties up and down beneath the trees, speaking little to each other, but apparently absorbed in the universal flood of business.

Many droschkies are prancing along the parade, harnessed with two horses in the old Russian style, one horse in the shafts and the other, dressé à volée, running loose at the side. This, at Petersburg and Moscow most aristocratic style of equipage in use, and singularly enough still used in all towns of any note by the chief of police, is surrendered at Nijny to the women of the demimonde.

We have still a few hours to loiter away before our train leaves for Moscow, and we take another run round the fair, noting some of the different lines and the goods they contain; here is one line all drugs and chemicals; here another for the sale of skins; silver goods have a line to themselves; and so on, all orderly arranged, well kept and clean swept.

Mounting a convenient church-tower we take a parting bird's-eye view of the place, lying on an angle of land formed by the junction of the Oka and the Volga, and so supplied with miles of wharfage by the banks of the two crowded rivers.

The last thing we turn to see, having still a few minutes to dispose of, is a circus, where we are sure to find a number of Tartar women among the audience; and there they are in fact so closely enveloped in shawls that it is difficult to understand how they can see anything or endure the heat of the place.

But the engine whistles, the train is ready, and we have to take our places in haste. In the railway Europe and Asia shake down together; a party of six Mussulmans from Bokhara go through long devotions soon after starting, praying no doubt to the Prophet to protect their wandering steps among the infidels of the West; and looking forward no doubt to a speedy return from these ends of the world to their own home again. We, on the other hand, anticipate our arrival in five days or so at Charing Cross or Cannon Street Station.

Now I have written down my observations in this fair the more lengthily that it is possible that the glories of Nijny are destined to an early diminution. Just now it is the greatest and most wonderful trade gathering in the world, where during the two months of its continuance upwards of 200,000 people circulate about seventeen millions of pounds sterling, mostly in direct purchase and sale of commodities lying on the spot between the buyer and seller; a system that time has destroyed in all other great marts and exchanges,—a system that the advance of railways will probably soon upset at Nijny, where however from its unique position, on the frontier of two worlds so to speak, a greater variety of produce and of purchasers assemble than could be gathered in any other one place in the world, and where for forty-five years prices of certain commodities have been dictated to the rest of Europe.

CHAPTER XI.

THE CENTRAL ASIAN QUESTION.

IN making a few remarks upon what is termed the encroachments of Russia in the Asiatic provinces bordering upon our north-western Indian frontier, I must dwell for a moment upon the proceedings of the Imperial Government of former days, as well as of the Khans themselves, in order more correctly to arrive at the position of the question of to-day.

The first recorded official act is, that the Khivans sent an ambassador to Ivan the Terrible in 1557, asking leave for their traders to barter with the Russians, and they followed this up by sending other envoys during the latter portion of the sixteenth century.

At the commencement of the seventeenth century, the Khivans complained of the inroads of the Oural Cossacks, who had taken advantage of their trading facilities to absolutely conquer Khiva; but they did not long enjoy their triumph, and were soon conquered in their turn.

In 1622, the Khan being again alive to his own interests, sought protection from the Czar Michael, but it was not until 1702, that, in answer to a petition sent to Peter the Great, that Czar took the Khan under his "protection," and received the allegiance of the Khivans.

Peter the Great, then, it was, who first showed a desire to open up through these steppes a route which his subjects could use to trade with India, as in 1715 he dispatched a party, *viâ* Khiva, to trade with India; and it will not be out of place to mention here, as helping to show what Peter's idea was, that about the same time he also sent a trading party to China.

This monarch also, a few years after, dispatched another envoy to the Khan, who however did not do any good, was finally murdered, and his suite were sold for slaves.

The object more particularly desired by this embassy, was to find out the truth of the reports which had been conveyed to Peter, relating to the riches in gold which were stated to be lying on the banks of the Oxus. Subsequent researches did not verify the statements, and on Peter's decease the relations between Russia and Khiva remained pretty much as they had been before, namely, continual receptions of envoys from the Khans for the purpose of making trading treaties, which were no sooner made than they were broken by the Khivans.

One important act may, however, be attributed to Peter the Great, and that was, he commenced the building of the trading forts on these Asiatic frontiers, at Semipalatinsk in 1718, under the strong feeling of the absolute necessity of opening up this quarter of the world to his traders.

The succeeding monarchs, Elizabeth and Catherine II., received more envoys, always with the same stories and the same results, and, about the year 1800, not only did these overtures of the Khivans terminate, but they actually threw over all pretended allegiance to the Czars of Russia by electing as Khan a prince who refused to have anything whatever to do with the Russians, and, in fact, began to commit depredations on the Russian frontier. This policy came to a climax in 1802, when the Khivans refused to allow a Russian envoy to pass through their country on a mission to Bokhara.

This country had for years been more friendly to the Russians; probably being farther from them there was not the same reason for the disputes which were always springing up with the Khivans.

The Emperor Paul, in the face of these proceedings of the Khivans, ordered the seizure of Khiva, and for this purpose assembled an army of 50,000 men at Orenburg, to make the campaign.

Paul dying just at this time, his warlike intentions were frustrated, and his successor, Alexander, who at first intended to carry out the project, altered his mind, and disbanded the Orenburg army.

In 1835, however, active operations were again commenced, and in 1839 the Emperor Nicholas dispatched an army and issued his memorable Orenburg Manifesto. In 1840, the Khan came to his senses, and during 1842 the first real working treaty was concluded with Russia and Khiva. Continual bickerings, however, still occurred. For several years a sort of guerilla warfare was kept up, and it was not until the year 1856 that the country could be considered as moderately quiet.

The Khans of Bokhara had sent many envoys to Russia during the commencement of the present century, always with one object,—to persuade the Russians to trade with them; both the Khanates of Bokhara and Khiva, and indirectly Khokand, depended absolutely upon receiving many of the commodities they most required—such as metals, dyes, hardware, gold, &c.—from Russia, and this fact alone made them endeavour to cultivate the good offices of the Russians, although their continual internal warfare and neighbouring jealousies made it a very difficult matter for the Russians to conduct any barter trade with them.

From the foregoing historical sketch what can be gathered? Are we justified in saying that the Russian policy has been leading up to the attempted conquest of India? My opinion is we are not. In the first place all the transactions with these Khans go to show that it was they who wished to enter into trading relations with the Russians, not the Russians who wished to subjugate them, and I believe nobody can suppose that Peter the Great or Catherine II. could have had any idea of conquering India or any part of it. Peter's mind was far too commercial for him not to see that even if such a feat were accomplished, he would ruin his already formed plans of consolidating his own country, and most certainly Catherine II.

was far too anxious to possess Turkey, to turn her attention seriously to the conquest of India; this was shown to be the case by the fact, that immediately after the Crimea had been declared independent of Turkey by the treaty of Kanardiz, and Catherine had taken that Khan under her "protection," the conquest of Constantinople was declared to be the policy of Russia.

There was a sound reason for the Russians primarily looking to the Central Asian provinces as an outlet for their commerce; and a sounder one for looking with coveting eyes on India as a place of trade; but it would appear that only the later monarchs of Russia paid much attention to this idea of Indian commerce, as after Peter's first essay before mentioned, nothing further seems to have been attempted with India direct until many years afterwards. I cannot, however, see any historical facts to prove those assertions which are so frequently made, that Russia's traditional policy has been, and is, the conquest of India; on the contrary, I contend that all facts show that policy is one of trade and commerce only.

Even the Asiatic deserts, boasting as they do of some of the most fertile oases in the world, could produce many articles valuable to Russia. Cotton, an article of great importance for Russia to receive from her own possessions, or overland *viâ* a tributary state, is one of those necessities which every nation would strive to acquire; and there is no reason why, with Bokhara quiet, it should not supply sufficient of this staple for all the Russian looms.

Many other useful productions, as silk, &c., could also be expected in quantity, and all these would help to balance the trade that must ensue by these people becoming buyers of Russian manufactures.

As I have before remarked in this book, the manufactures of Russia are more suited for Eastern marts than any others; it is a well known fact that for them a particular fashion is necessary, which fashion the Russian manufacturers excel in, the Asiatic taste has become moulded on many of their productions, and they find in these people their best customers. It was not only then these provinces that would so directly benefit the Russians, but the much extended trade that they might expect to inaugurate with countries of whose conquest they could never hope.

Through what is called Little Bokhara, Russia could open a way to a part of that mighty Celestial Empire, whose enormous population might be counted upon with certainty to demand a host of Russian manufactured articles, and who, in return, could supply her with raw materials far more facilely than by the extreme north-eastern route of Maimatchin and Kiatchta. India was a golden opportunity; did she not produce indigo, cotton, coffee, and drugs? The very neediest necessities for such an Empire as Russia. Was not this an opening that could not be lost to a people gradually waking to commercial views?

In exchange for these invaluable commodities, Russia would barter with her cloths and cotton goods, cutlery, and knick-knacks, and thus keep a splendid trade in her own hands.

In spite of all I constantly read, I here wish to record the fact, that Russia can and does compete with other European manufacturers in several articles—cloth, for instance,—the Russian sends this overland to China across the circuitous Kiachta route, and sells it in Pekin cheaper than the English can, though their cloth goes across the sea instead of the land.

Again the Russians are, from necessity, a great carrying people; perhaps no people in the world understand this business so well, or do it so cheaply, and they would naturally look to the great benefit to be derived from the transport of Indian goods. Once subjugate these Asiatic hordes in the lowlands, and they might hope to carry a mass of goods—Indian for England, and English for India. This could not be attempted with the present difficulties in the way; but it is quite possible to utilize the Sir Daria and Amu Daria, and by these means of navigation to bring the price for transit down to a reasonable figure; even now, with land carriage, the whole distance excepting a short journey on the Volga from Samara to Nijny Novgorod, silk can be brought from Bokhara to St. Petersburg for 2d. per pound.

I maintain then that the commercial interests of Russia negative the assertion of those who state she has an eye on our Oriental jewel — from a military point of view, it seems to me more improbable still. Russia, with her eighty millions of square miles of territory, has at least a sufficient frontier to guard, without placing the mountains of India between a half-conquered horde of savages and her own territory. Her soldiers are of all nations the most unsuited to an Indian climate, and such an exploit as sending an army the other side of the Hindu Kush, would be only a repetition of Napoleon's march to Moscow, and with the same result.

Russia could not administer such a country as India—she has not the people fit for it. It took England years before she could even educate a staff, which after all, then did little better than misrule instead of govern.

Again, before the Russians could reach British India, the Affghans must be settled with, an undertaking by itself which the Russians would be unwilling to attempt, and undesirable also, when the roaming inhabitants of the Khanates would be between them and their base of operations.

If the Russians had this idea of conquest, why should they have taken the trouble to go through these different Khanates, when they could get to India in less time from the Caspian than they could from Bokhara, and with this advantage, that the Caspian would be a safe base of operations.

It may be true, as M. Vambery says, that Russian monarchs are carrying out the idea for the formation of the great Tartar kingdom as imagined by Ivan Vassilyvitch, in 1500, by annexing the three Khanates; but

I again repeat and maintain, that there is no excuse for asserting that Russia has any designs upon India, and that commercially, politically, and from a military point of view, it is impossible she should entertain any such wishes.

It is without doubt difficult in Russia for the people to arrive at the policy of their Government, as no public discussions arise upon the intentions of their Ruler, or the wishes of the Ministry; but from what may be gathered from the press, the general opinion is, that the Government exercised a wise discretion in taming these uncivilized hordes, with the sole idea of benefiting national trade, but all ridicule the notion of an advance upon India, both upon military and commercial grounds.

Touching what has actually been done by Russians in Central Asia, the Russians fail to see any other policy than that of England in

India. They point out the truth of the remark of one of their able writers who said, " The English in Asia represented the commencement of civilization and humanity, they put an end to the reign of brigandage and replaced it by one of justice and order; the English have been the saviours of India, they appear as the defenders of the rights of humanity; the bloody era terminates with the conquest of the English, and though their government has not been an example of perfection, it is impossible not to admit that it has been decidedly more mild, humane, and just, than any other government under which Hindoos have ever lived."

This, then, is a Russian tribute to our proceedings in India, and Russia claims a similar acknowledgment for her humanizing influence in those Asiatic steppes, where, through her means, Christianity has already broken the chains of the most bigoted Mahommedanism, the most blind intolerance, and the most lascivious life that was probably to be found in any nation in the world.

CHAPTER XII.

CONCLUSION.

I HAVE, in the preceding pages, attempted to give a fair account of the existing state of affairs in Russia. I wish to conclude by mentioning a few general impressions.

In endeavouring to show the good side of the subjects treated upon, I have not shut my eyes to that reverse of the picture which still, in many cases, undoubtedly exists. I look upon Russia as a country now going through that crisis which must always occur in the history of every great nation, when it is changing from a state of backwardness and sluggishness to one of progress, and when the intelligence and honesty of the country are combatting with the ignorance and narrow-mindedness of the retrogrades.

Amongst the institutions—the police, for instance—whose very name used to be a bugbear to all classes, are now a decent and respectably behaved class, and although not particularly active they attend fairly to their proper duties.

The press, not free, but as much so as that of France under Napoleon the Third, discusses pretty liberally the politics of the day.

A considerable improvement is to be noticed amongst the priests; they are decidedly better looked after, and a better educated class of men is appearing amongst them.

The young nobles are no longer brought up with the idea of the positive necessity of " serving ; " as a result, many an educated young man now turns his attention to other matters besides the glory of the Imperial Eagle — becomes a resident on his estate, and looks after the management himself, instead of leaving the same to the tender mercies of some rascally Russo-Germanic intendant. The benefit conferred upon the local population by these resident landlords is immense.

The cry for education has at length been raised. The people are awakening to the fact that knowledge is as necessary to a man as his daily bread.

Russia has a future before her so great, that no man can realise what she may become; whether her power will be used for good or for evil must depend on the minds of her future rulers. With peace, she holds in her hands a destiny unequalled for its greatness in the pages of history; let us hope that future generations will admit that this destiny has been wielded for the good of mankind.

The people have much to thank their present ruler for, who, by his own will, through his choice of able and honest advisers, has done so much for them.

When called away from his sphere of usefulness, history shall record and recount the goodness of heart of Alexander Nicholaievitch. When those who are now children read the pages which will tell them who they have to thank for the benefits that they enjoy, the whole civilized world will join in bearing witness to the justice of the prayer, which now nearly thirty millions of emancipated serfs offer up to their Maker, when they daily say :—

"God bless our Lord the Czar!"

THE END.